Travellers' Italian

David Ellis is Director of the Somerset Language Centre and co-author of a number of language books

Cinzia Mariella was born in Turin and now works in London teaching Italian to adults

Dr John Baldwin is Lecturer in Phonetics at University College, London

Other titles in the series

Travellers' **Dutch**
Travellers' **French**
Travellers' **German**
Travellers' **Greek**
Travellers' **Italian**
Travellers' **Japanese**
Travellers' **Portuguese**
Travellers' **Scandinavian**
Travellers' **Serbo-Croat** (for Yugoslavia)
Travellers' **Spanish**
Travellers' **Multilingual Phrase Book**

Travellers' Italian

D. L. Ellis, C. Mariella

Pronunciation **Dr J. Baldwin**

Pan Books London, Sydney and Auckland

The publishers would like to thank the Italian State Tourist
Office (ENIT) for their help during the preparation of this book.

First published 1981 by Pan Books Ltd,
Cavaye Place, London SW10 9PG
19 18 17 16 15 14
© D. L. Ellis and C. Mariella 1981
ISBN 0 330 26295 5
Printed and bound in Great Britain by
Richard Clay Ltd, Bungay, Suffolk

Contents

6/Contents

Using the phrase book

- This phrase book is designed to help you get by in Italy, to get what you want or need. It concentrates on the simplest but most effective way you can express these needs in an unfamiliar language.
- The CONTENTS on p. 5 give you a good idea of which section to consult for the phrase you need.
- The INDEX on p. 153 gives you more detailed information about where to look for your phrase.
- When you have found the right page you will be given:
  either – the exact phrase
  or   – help in making up a suitable sentence
  and   – help in getting the pronunciation right
- The English sentences in **bold** type will be useful for you in a variety of different situations, so they are worth learning by heart. (See also DO IT YOURSELF, p. 143.)
- Wherever possible you will find help in understanding what Italian people say to *you* in reply to your questions.
- If you want to practise the basic nuts and bolts of the language further, look at the DO IT YOURSELF section starting on p. 143.
- Note especially these three sections:
  Everyday expressions p. 11
  Shop talk p. 57
  Public notices p. 123
  You are sure to want to refer to them most frequently.
- When you arrive in Italy make good use of the tourist information offices (see p. 24).
  UK addresses: Italian State Tourist Office (ENIT)
  201 Regent Street, London W1R 8AY
  47 Merrion Square, Dublin 2.

A note on the pronunciation system

It is usual in phrase books for there to be a pronunciation section, which tries to teach English-speaking tourists how to pronounce correctly the language of the country they are visiting. Such attempts are based on the argument that correct pronunciation is essential for comprehension. The system in this book, however, is founded on three quite different assumptions: firstly, that it is not possible to describe in print the sounds of a foreign language in such a way that the English speaker with no phonetic training will produce them accurately, or even intelligibly; secondly, that perfect pronunciation is not essential for communication; and lastly, that the average visitor abroad is more interested in achieving successful communication than in learning how to pronounce new speech sounds. Observation and experience have shown these assumptions to be justified. The most important characteristic of the present system, therefore, is that it makes no attempt whatsoever to teach the sounds of the other language, but uses instead the nearest English sounds to them. The sentences transcribed for pronunciation are designed to be read as naturally as possible, as if they were ordinary English (of a generally South-Eastern English variety), and with no attempt to make the words sound 'foreign'. In this way you will still sound quite English but you will at the same time be understood. Practice always helps performance and it is a good idea to rehearse aloud any of the sentences you know you are going to need. When you do come to the point of using them, say them with conviction.

In Italian it is important to stress, or emphasize the syllables in *italics*, just as you would if we were to take as an English example: little Jack H*o*rner s*a*t in the c*o*rner. Here we have ten syllables, but only four stresses. This Italian sentence also has ten syllables but only four stresses: qu*e*sta m*a*cchina è rumor*o*sa (this car is noisy).

Of course you may enjoy trying to pronounce a foreign language as well as possible and the present system is a good way to start. However, since it uses only the sounds of English, you will very soon need to depart from it as you imitate the sounds you hear the native speaker produce and begin to relate them to the spelling of the other language. Italian will pose no problems as there is an obvious and consistent relationship between pronunciation and spelling.

Divertitevi! *John Baldwin, 1980*

Regions and regional capitals

Switzerland

VALLE
D'ASTA
Aosta

France

Austria

ALTO ADIGE

Torino

LOMBARDIA

Trento • Bolzano

PIEMONTE

Milano

TRENTINO

FRIULI-
VENEZIA-
GIULIA

LIGURIA • Genova

VENETO

Trieste

Venezia

Jugoslavia

EMILIA-
ROMAGNA

• Bologna

Firenze •

Elba

TOSCANA

Perugia •

• Ancona

Giglio •

UMBRIA

LE MARCHE

LAZIO

SARDEGNA

• L'Aquila

Roma •

ABRUZZI

Tremiti
Islands

• Cagliari

MOLISE

• Campobasso

Ischia •

• Napoli

Capri •

CAMPANIA

Potenza •

• Bari

Egadi
Islands

LUCANIA

PUGLIA

Lipari
Islands

• Palermo

CALABRIA

Catanzaro •

N

SICILIA

0   km   150

Everyday expressions

[See also 'Shop talk', p. 57.]

Hello ⎤	**Buon giorno**
	boo-*on* jorno
Good morning	**Ciao** (friends only)
Good day (before lunch) ⎦	chow
Good afternoon (after lunch) ⎤	**Buona sera**
Good evening ⎦	boo-*ona* s*e*h-ra
Good night	**Buona notte**
	boo-*ona* n*o*t-teh
Good-bye	**A rivederci**
	ah reeveh-d*ai*rchee
See you later	**A più tardi**
	ah pew t*a*rdee
Yes	**Sí**
	see
Please	**Per favore**
	pair fav-*o*reh
Yes, please	**Sí grazie**
	s*e*e gr*a*tzee-eh
Great!	**Magnifico!**
	man-y*ee*feeco
Thank you	**Grazie**
	gr*a*tzee-eh
Thank you very much	**Molte grazie**
	m*o*lteh gr*a*tzee-eh
That's right	**Esatto**
	ez*a*t-to
No	**No**
	noh
No thank you	**No, grazie**
	n*o*h gr*a*tzee-eh
I disagree	**Non sono d'accordo**
	non sonno dak-k*o*rdo
Excuse me ⎤	**Scusi**
Sorry ⎦	sc*oo*zee
Don't mention it ⎤	**Prego**
That's OK ⎦	pr*e*g-o

That's good I like it	**Va bene** va ben-eh
That's no good I don't like it	**Non va bene** non va ben-eh
I know	**Lo so** lo so
I don't know	**Non lo so** non lo so
It doesn't matter	**Non importa** non importa
Where's the toilet, please?	**Dov'è il bagno, per favore?** dov-eh il ban-yo pair fav-oreh
How much is that? [*point*]	**Quanto costa?** quanto costa
Is the service included?	**Il servizio è compreso?** il sairvizio eh compraizo
Do you speak English?	**Parla inglese?** parla inglaizeh
I'm sorry ...	**Mi dispiace ...** mee dispi-ah-cheh ...
I don't speak Italian	**non parlo italiano** non parlo italian-o
I only speak a little Italian	**parlo solo un poco italiano** parlo solo oon poco italian-o
I don't understand	**non capisco** non capisco
Please can you ...	**Per favore potrebbe ...** pair fav-oreh potreb-beh ...
repeat that?	**ripetere?** ripet-ereh
speak more slowly?	**parlare piú lentamente?** parlar-eh pew lentamenteh
write it down?	**scriverlo?** screeverlo
What is this called in Italian? [*point*]	**Come si dice questo in italiano?** com-eh see deecheh questo in italian-o

Crossing the border

ESSENTIAL INFORMATION

- Don't waste time just before you leave rehearsing what you're going to say to the border officials – the chances are that you won't have to say anything at all, especially if you travel by air.
- It's more useful to check that you have your documents handy for the journey: passport, tickets, money, travellers' cheques, insurance documents, driving licence and car registration documents.
- Look out for these signs:

ALT!	(stop!)
CONTROLLO PASSAPORTI	(passport control)
DOGANA	(customs)
POLIZIA DI FRONTIERA	(border police)
FRONTIERA	(border)

  [For further signs and notices see p. 123.]
- You may be asked routine questions by the customs officials [see below]. If you have to give personal details see 'Meeting people', p. 14. The other important answer to know is 'Nothing':
  Niente (nee-enteh).

ROUTINE QUESTIONS

Passport?	**Passaporto?**
	pas-saporto
Insurance?	**Assicurazione?**
	as-sicooratzioneh
Registration document? (logbook)	**Libretto di circolazione?**
	libret-to dee cheercolatzi-oneh
Ticket, please	**Biglietto, prego**
	bil-yet-to preg-o
Have you anything to declare?	**Ha niente da dichiarare?**
	ah nee-enteh da dikee-arar-eh
Where are you going?	**Dove va?**
	dov-eh va
How long are you staying?	**Per quanto tempo rimane?**
	pair quanto tempo reeman-eh
Where have you come from?	**Da dove viene?**
	da dov-eh vee-ehneh

You may also have to fill in forms which ask for:

surname	**cognome**
first name	**nome**
date of birth	**data di nascita**
place of birth	**luogo di nascita**
address	**indirizzo**
nationality	**nazionalità**
profession	**professione**
passport number	**numero passaporto**
issued at	**emesso a**
signature	**firma**

Meeting people

[See also 'Everyday expressions', p. 11.]

Breaking the ice

Hello ⎤ Good morning ⎦ How are you?	**Buon giorno (Ciao)** boo-*on* j*o*rno (chow) **Come sta? (Come stai?)** com-eh st*a* (com-eh st*a*-ee)

(Expressions above in parenthesis should only be used with people you know well.)

Pleased to meet you	**Piacere** pee-ach*ai*reh
I am here ...	**Sono qui ...** s*o*nno quee ...
on holiday	**in vacanza** in vac-*a*ntza
on business	**per affari** pair aff*a*r-ee
Can I offer you ...	**Posso offrirle ...** p*o*s-so offr*ee*r-leh ...
a drink?	**da bere?** da b*ai*reh
a cigarette?	**una sigaretta?** oona sigar*et*-ta

a cigar?	**un sigaro?**
	oon s*i*garo
Are you staying long?	**Rimane per molto?**
	reem*a*n-eh pair m*o*lto

Name

What's your name?	**Come si chiama?**
	c*o*m-eh see kee-*a*m-ah
My name is ...	**Mi chiamo ...**
	mee kee-*a*m-o ...

Family

Are you married?	**Lei è sposato/a***
	lay eh spoz*a*t-o/-ah
I am ...	**Sono ...**
	s*o*nno ...
married	**sposato/a***
	spoz*a*t-o/-ah
single	**da sposare**
	da spoz*a*r-eh
This is ...	**Le presento ...**
	leh pres*e*nto ...
my wife	**mia moglie**
	mee-ah m*o*l-yeh
my husband	**mio marito**
	mee-o mar*ee*to
my son	**mio figlio**
	mee-o f*ee*l-yo
my daughter	**mia figlia**
	mee-ah f*ee*l-ya
my (boy) friend	**il mio ragazzo**
	il mee-o rag*a*t-tzo
my (girl) friend	**la mia ragazza**
	la mee-ah rag*a*t-tza
my (male) colleague	**il mio collega**
	il mee-o col-*le*g-ah
my (female) colleague	**la mia collega**
	la mee-ah col-*le*g-ah

* For men use 'o', for women use 'a'.

Do you have any children?	Lei ha bambini?
	lay ah bambeenee
I have ...	Ho ...
	o ...
one daughter	una figlia
	oona feel-ya
one son	un figlio
	oon feel-yo
two daughters	due figlie
	dooeh feel-yeh
three sons	tre figli
	treh feel-yee
No, I haven't any children	No, non ho bambini
	noh non o bambeenee

Where you live

Are you ...	Lei è ...
	lay eh ...
Italian?	italiano/a?*
	italian-o/-ah
Swiss?	svizzero/a?*
	svit-tzero/ah
I am ...	Sono ...
	sonno ...
American	americano/a*
	american-o/-ah
English	inglese
	inglaizeh

[For other nationalities, see p. 136]

I live ...	Abito ...
	ah-beeto ...
in London	a Londra
	ah londra
in England	in Inghilterra
	in ing-ill-tairra

[For other countries see p. 136.]

* For men use 'o', for women use 'a'.

in the north	**al nord**
	al nord
in the south	**al sud**
	al sood
in the east	**all'est**
	al-laist
in the west	**all'ovest**
	al-lovaist
in the centre	**al centro**
	al chentro

For the businessman and woman

I'm from ... (firm's name)	**Sono della ...**
	sonno del-la ...
I have an appointment with ...	**Ho un appuntamento con ...**
	o oon ap-poontamento con ...
May I speak to ... ?	**Potrei parlare con ... ?**
	potray parlar-eh con ...
This is my card	**Ecco il mio biglietto da visita**
	ec-co il mee-o bil-yet-to da vizita
I'm sorry, I'm late	**Mi dispiace, sono in ritardo**
	mee dispi-ah-cheh sonno in reetardo
Can I fix another appointment?	**Potrei fissare un altro appuntamento?**
	potray fis-sar-eh oon altro ap-poontamento
I'm staying at the (Paris) Hotel	**Sono all'hotel (Parigi)**
	sonno al-lotel (par-eejee)
I'm staying in (St John's) Road	**Sto in via (San Giovanni)**
	sto in vee-ah (san jovan-nee)

Asking the way

ESSENTIAL INFORMATION

● Keep a look-out for all these place names as you will find them on shops, maps and notices.

WHAT TO SAY

Excuse me, please	**Scusi, per favore**
	s*coo*zee, pair fav-*o*reh
How do I get ...	**Per andare ...**
	pair and*a*r-eh ...
to Rome?	**a Roma?**
	ah r*o*ma
to the Via Nomentana?	**in via Nomentana?**
	in vee-ah noment*a*n-ah
to the Hotel Torino?	**all'hotel Torino?**
	al-lot-*e*l tor*ee*no
to the airport?	**all'aeroporto?**
	al-la-airop*o*rto
to the beach?	**alla spiaggia?**
	al-la spee-*a*d-ja
to the bus station?	**alla stazione degli autobus?**
	al-la statz*io*neh del-yee ah-*oo*tobus
to the historic site?	**al centro storico?**
	al ch*e*ntro st*o*rico
to the market?	**al mercato?**
	al mairc*a*t-o
to the police station?	**alla stazione di polizia?**
	al-la statz*io*neh dee politz*ee*-ah
to the port?	**al porto?**
	al p*o*rto
to the post office?	**all'ufficio postale?**
	al-loof-*fee*cho post*a*l-eh
to the railway station?	**alla stazione ferroviaria?**
	al-la statz*io*neh ferrovee-*a*r-ee-ah
to the sports stadium?	**allo stadio?**
	al-lo st*a*d-*ee*o

to the tourist information office?	**all'ufficio informazioni turistiche?**
	al-loof-*fee*cho informatzi*o*nee toor*i*stikeh
to the town centre?	**in centro?**
	in ch*e*ntro
to the town hall?	**al Municipio?**
	al moonich*ee*-peeo
Excuse me, please	**Scusi, per favore**
	sc*oo*zee pair fav-*o*reh
Is there . . . nearby?	**C'è . . . qui vicino?**
	cheh . . . quee veech*ee*no
an art gallery	**una galleria d'arte**
	*oo*na gal-ler*ee*-ah d*a*rteh
a baker's	**una panetteria**
	*oo*na panet-ter*ee*-ah
a bank	**una banca**
	*oo*na b*a*nca
a bar	**un bar**
	oon bar
a botanical garden	**un giardino botanico**
	oon jard*ee*no bot*a*n-eeco
a bus stop	**una fermata d'autobus**
	*oo*na fairm*a*t-ah d*a-oo*tobus
a butcher's	**una macelleria**
	*oo*na machel-ler*ee*-ah
a café	**un caffè**
	oon caf-f*e*h
a cake shop	**una pasticceria**
	*oo*na pasteet-chair*ee*-ah
a campsite	**un campeggio**
	oon camp*e*d-jo
a car park	**un parcheggio**
	oon park*e*d-jo
a change bureau	**un ufficio del cambio**
	oon oof-*fee*cho del c*a*mbeeo
a chemist's	**una farmacia**
	*oo*na farmach*ee*-ah
a church	**una chiesa**
	*oo*na kee-*e*hza
a cinema	**un cinema**
	oon ch*e*enema

Is there . . . nearby?	C'è . . . qui vicino?
	cheh . . . quee veech*ee*no
a delicatessen	una salumeria
	oona saloomer*ee*-ah
a dentist's	un dentista
	oon dent*ee*sta
a department store	un grande magazzino
	oon gr*a*ndeh magad-dz*ee*no
a disco	una discoteca
	oona discot*ec*-ah
a doctor's surgery	uno studio medico
	oono st*oo*dio med-*ee*co
a dry-cleaner's	una lavanderia a secco
	oona lavander*ee*-ah ah s*e*c-co
a fishmonger's	una pescheria
	oona pesker*ee*-ah
a garage (for repairs)	un' autoriparazioni
	oon a-ootoriparatzi-*o*nee
a hairdresser's	un parrucchiere
	oon par-rooc-kee-*ai*reh
a greengrocer's	un verduriere
	oon vairdoo-ree-*ai*reh
a grocer's	un alimentari
	oon alimen-t*a*r-ee
a hardware shop	un negozio di ferramenta
	oon neg*o*tzio dee ferram*e*nta
a Health and Social Security Office	una sezione dell'INAM
	oona setzi*o*neh del-l*ee*nam
a hospital	un ospedale
	oon osped*a*l-eh
a hotel	un hotel
	oon ot*e*l
an ice-cream parlour	una gelateria
	oona jelat-cr*ee*-ah
a laundry	una lavanderia
	oona lavander*ee*-ah
a museum	un museo
	oon mooz*e*h-o
a newsagent's	un'edicola
	oonede*e*cola

a night club	**un night**
	oon night
a petrol station	**un distributore**
	oon distribootoreh
a post box	**una buca per lettere**
	oona booca pair let-tereh
a public garden (town park)	**un giardino pubblico**
	oon jardeeno poob-blico
a restaurant	**un ristorante**
	oon ristoranteh
a (snack) bar	**un bar**
	oon bar
a sports ground	**un campo sportivo**
	oon campo sporteevo
a supermarket	**un supermercato**
	oon sooper-maircat-o
a sweet shop	**una pasticceria**
	oona pasteet-chairee-ah
a swimming pool	**una piscina**
	oona pisheena
a taxi stand	**una stazione taxi**
	oona statzioneh taxi
a telephone	**un telefono**
	oon telephono
a theatre	**un teatro**
	oon teh-atro
a tobacconist's	**un tabaccaio**
	oon tabac-cah-yo
a toilet	**un gabinetto pubblico**
	oon gabinet-to poob-blico
a travel agent's	**un'agenzia di viaggi**
	oonajentzee-ah dee vee-ad-jee
a youth hostel	**un ostello per la gioventú**
	oon ostel-lo pair la joventoo
a zoo	**uno zoo**
	oono dzor

DIRECTIONS

- Asking where a place is, or if a place is nearby, is one thing; making sense of the answer is another.
- Here are some of the most important key directions and replies.

Left	**Sinistra** sineestra
Right	**Destra** destra
Straight on	**Sempre diritto** sempreh deereet-to
There	**Lá** la
First left/right	**La prima a sinistra/destra** la preema ah sineestra/destra
Second left/right	**La seconda a sinistra/destra** la seconda ah sineestra/destra
At the crossroads	**All'incrocio** alleencro-cho
At the traffic lights	**Al semaforo** al semaphoro
At the roundabout	**Alla rotonda** al-la rotonda
At the level crossing	**Al passaggio a livello** al pas-sad-jo ah leevel-lo
It's near/far	**È vicino/lontano** eh veecheeno/lontan-o
One kilometre	**Un chilometro** oon keelometro
Two kilometres	**Due chilometri** dooeh keelometree
Five minutes ...	**Cinque minuti ...** chinqueh minootee ...
on foot	**a piedi** ah pee-ehdee
by car	**in macchina** in mac-keena

Take ...	Prenda ...
	prenda ...
the bus	l'autobus
	la-*oo*tobus
the train	il treno
	il tren-o
the tram	il tram
	il tram
the underground	la metropolitana
	la metro-poleetan-ah

[*For public transport see p. 114.*]

The tourist information office

ESSENTIAL INFORMATION

- Most towns and even villages in Italy have a tourist information office, run by the regional or local tourist boards.
- Look for these words:
  UFFICIO INFORMAZIONI TURISTICHE
  ENTE TURISMO
- You can also get information from the Touring Club and Automobile Club offices, often indicated with the abbreviations **TCI** (Italian Touring Club) and **ACI** (Italian Automobile Club). **ACI** also offers help with car repairs or accidents.
- These offices give you free information in the form of printed leaflets, fold-outs, brochures, lists and plans.
- You may have to pay for some types of document, but this is not usual.
- For finding a tourist office, see p. 18.

WHAT TO SAY

Please have you got . . .
Per favore avete . . .
pair fav-*oreh* avet-eh . . .

a plan of the town?
una piantina della città?
oona pee-ant*eena* del-la chit-t*a*

a list of hotels?
un elenco degli alberghi?
oon elen-co del-yee alb*air*-ghee

a list of campsites?
un elenco dei campeggi?
oon elen-co day camped-jee

a list of restaurants?
un elenco dei ristoranti?
oon elen-co day ristor*antee*

a list of coach excursions?
un elenco di gite in autobus?
oon elen-co dee j*ee*teh in ah-*oo*toboos

a list of events?
un elenco di avvenimenti?
oon elen-co dee av-venim*entee*

a leaflet on the town?
un opuscolo sulla città?
oon op*oos*-colo sool-la chit-t*a*

a leaflet on the region?
un opuscolo sulla regione?
oon op*oos*-colo sool-la reh-j*oneh*

a railway timetable?	**un orario ferroviario?**
	oon or-*areeo* ferrovi-*ar*-eeo
a bus timetable?	**un orario degli autobus?**
	oon or*ar*-eeo d*el*-yee ah-*oo*toboos
In English, please	**In inglese, per favore**
	in ingl*ai*zeh pair fav-*o*reh
How much do I owe you?	**Quanto Le devo?**
	qu*ar*to leh d*ev*-o
Can you recommend ...	**Mi potrebbe raccomandare ...**
	mee potr*eb*-beh rac-comand*ar*-eh...
a cheap hotel?	**un albergo non caro?**
	oon alb*air*-go non c*ar*-o
a cheap restaurant?	**un ristorante non caro?**
	oon ristor*an*teh non c*ar*-o
Can you make a booking for me?	**Potrebbe prenotare per me?**
	potr*eb*-beh prenot-*ar*-eh pair m*eh*

LIKELY ANSWERS

You need to understand when the answer is 'No'. You should be able to tell by the assistant's facial expression, tone of voice and gesture, but there are some language clues, such as:

No	**No**
	noh
I'm sorry	**Mi dispiace**
	mee dispi-*ah*-cheh
I don't have a list of campsites	**Non ho un elenco dei campeggi**
	non o oon el*en*-co day camp*ed*-jee
I haven't got any left	**Non ne ho più**
	non neh o p*ew*
It's free	**È gratis**
	eh gr*at*-is

Accommodation

Hotel

ESSENTIAL INFORMATION

- If you want hotel-type accommodation, all the following words in capital letters are worth looking for on name boards:
  HOTEL
  ALBERGO] (hotel)
  MOTEL (two main chains are run by ACI and Agip)
  PENSIONE (boarding house)
- Hotels are divided into five classes (from luxury to tourist class) and **pensioni** into three.
- Lists of hotels and **pensioni** can be obtained from local tourist offices or ENIT in London [*see p. 24*].
- The cost is displayed in the room itself, so you can check it when having a look round before agreeing to stay.
- The displayed cost is for the room itself, per night and not per person. Breakfast is extra and therefore optional.
- Service and VAT are always included in the cost of the room, so tipping is voluntary.
- Not all hotels provide meals, apart from breakfast. A pensione always provides meals. Breakfast is continental-style: coffee or tea, with rolls and jam.
- An identity document is requested when registering at a hotel and will normally be kept overnight. Passports or driving licences are accepted.
- Finding a hotel, see p. 18.

WHAT TO SAY

I have a booking

Ho una prenotazione
o oona prenotatzi-*o*neh

Have you any vacancies, please?

Avete delle camere libere, per favore?
av*et*-eh del-leh *ca*mereh l*ee*bereh pair fav-*o*reh

Can I book a room?	**Potrei prenotare una camera?**
	potr*ay* prenot-*ar*-eh *oo*na *c*amera
It's for ...	**È per ...**
	eh pair ...
one person	**una persona**
	*oo*na pairs*o*na
two people	**due persone**
	d*oo*eh pairs*o*neh

[*For numbers see p.128.*]

It's for ...	**È per ...**
	eh pair ...
one night	**un:. notte**
	*oo*na n*o*t-teh
two nights	**due notti**
	d*oo*eh n*o*t-tee
one week	**una settimana**
	*oo*na set-tim*an*-ah
two weeks	**due settimane**
	d*oo*eh set-tim*an*-eh
I would like ...	**Vorrei ...**
	vorr*ay* ...
a room	**una camera**
	*oo*na *c*amera
two rooms	**due camere**
	d*oo*eh *c*amereh
with a single bed	**singola/e ***
	s*i*ngola/eh
with two single beds	**a due letti**
	ah d*oo*eh *l*et-tee
with a double bed	**con un letto matrimoniale**
	con oon *l*et-to matrimon-y*al*-eh
with a toilet] with a bathroom	**con bagno**
	con b*an*-yo
with a shower	**con doccia**
	con d*o*t-cha
with a cot	**con una culla**
	con oona *c*ool-la
with a balcony	**con terrazza**
	con terr*a*t-tza

* Use 'a' for one single bed, 'e' for two single beds.

I would like ...	**Vorrei ...**
	vorr*ay* ...
full board	**pensione completa**
	pen-see*o*neh complet-ah
half board	**mezza pensione**
	med-dza pen-see*o*neh
bed and breakfast	**solo colazione**
[see Essential information]	solo colatzioneh

Do you serve meals?	**Servite i pasti?**
	sairv*ee*teh ee p*a*stee
At what time is ...	**A che ora è ...**
	ah keh ora *eh* ...
breakfast?	**la colazione?**
	la colatzioneh
lunch?	**il pranzo?**
	il pr*a*ntzo
dinner?	**la cena?**
	la ch*e*n-ah
How much is it?	**Quanto costa?**
	qu*a*nto costa
Can I look at the room?	**Potrei vedere la stanza?**
	potr*ay* ved-*ai*reh la st*a*ntza
I'd prefer a room	**Preferirei una stanza ...**
	prefairee-r*ay* oona st*a*ntza ...
at the front/at the back	**sul davanti/sul retro**
	sool dav*a*ntee/sool retro
I'd like a quiet room	**Vorrei una camera tranquilla**
	vorr*ay* *oo*na camera tranqu*ee*l-la
OK, I'll take it	**Va bene, la prendo**
	va ben-eh la pr*e*ndo
No thanks, I won't take it	**No grazie, non la prendo**
	n*o*h gr*a*tzee-eh non la pr*e*ndo
The key to number (10), please	**Per favore la chiave del numero (dieci)**
	pair fav-*o*reh la kee-*a*hveh del n*oo*mero (dee-*e*chee)
Please may I have ...	**Per favore, potrei avere ...**
	pair fav-*o*reh potr*ay* av*ai*reh ..
a coat hanger?	**un attaccapanni?**
	oon at-tac-cap*a*n-nee

a towel?	**un asciugamano?**
	oon ashoogam*a*n-o
a glass?	**un bicchiere?**
	oon beec-kee-*ai*reh
some soap?	**del sapone?**
	del sapon*e*h
an ashtray?	**un portacenere?**
	oon portach*ai*nereh
another pillow?	**un altro cuscino?**
	oon *a*ltro coosh*ee*no
another blanket?	**un'altra coperta?**
	oon*a*ltra cop*ai*rta
Come in!	**Avanti!**
	av*a*ntee
One moment, please!	**Un momento, per favore!**
	oon mom*e*nto pair fav-*o*reh
Please can you ...	**Per favore, potrebbe ...**
	pair fav-*o*reh potr*e*b-beh ...
do this laundry/dry-cleaning?	**far lavare questo/far lavare questo a secco?**
	far lav*a*r-eh qu*e*sto/far lav*a*r-eh qu*e*sto ah s*e*c-co
call me at ...?	**chiamarmi alle ...?**
	kee-am*a*rmee *a*l-leh ...
help me with my luggage?	**aiutarmi con i bagagli?**
	ah-yoot*a*rmee con ee bag*a*l-yee
call be a taxi for ...?	**chiamarmi un taxi per le ...?**
	kee-am*a*rmee oon taxi pair leh ...

[*For times see p. 130.*]

The bill, please	**Il conto, per favore**
	il c*o*nto pair fav-*o*reh
Is service included?	**Il servizio è compreso?**
	il sairv*í*tzio eh compr*ai*zo
I think this is wrong	**Penso che questo sia sbagliato**
	p*e*nso keh qu*e*sto s*ee*-ah sbal-y*a*t-o
May I have a receipt?	**Potrei avere una ricevuta?**
	potr*a*y av*ai*reh oona reechev*oo*ta

At breakfast

Some more ... please	**Ancora ... per favore**
	ancora ... pair fav-*o*reh
coffee	**del caffè**
	del caf-*f*eh
tea	**del tè**
	del *t*eh
bread	**del pane**
	del p*a*n-eh
butter	**del burro**
	del b*oo*rro
jam	**della marmellata**
	del-la marmel-*l*at-ah
May I have a boiled egg?	**Potrei avere un uovo à la coque?**
	potr*a*y av*ai*reh oon w*o*v-o ah la coc

LIKELY REACTIONS

Have you an identity document, please?	**Ha un documento di riconoscimento, per favore?**
	ah oon doc*oo*mento dee riconosh*ee*mento pair fav-*o*reh
What's your name? [*see p. 15*]	**Come si chiama?**
	c*o*m-eh see kee-*a*m-ah
Sorry, we're full	**Spiacente, siamo al completo**
	spee-ach*e*nteh see-*a*m-o al compl*e*t-o
I haven't any rooms left	**Non ci sono piú camere**
	non chee s*o*nno pew c*a*mereh
Do you want to have a look?	**Vuole vederla?**
	voo-*o*leh ved-*ai*rla
How many people is it for?	**Per quante persone?**
	pair qu*a*nteh pairs*o*neh
From (seven o'clock) onwards	**Dalle (sette) in poi**
	d*a*l-leh (s*e*t-teh) in poy
From (midday) onwards	**Da (mezzogiorno) in poi**
	da (med-dzoj*o*rno) in poy
[*For times see p. 130.*]	
It's (10,000) lira	**Fa (diecimila) lire**
	fa (dee-*e*chee m*ee*la) l*ee*reh
[*For numbers see p. 128.*]	

Camping and youth hostelling

ESSENTIAL INFORMATION

Camping

- Look for the words: **CAMPING** or **CAMPEGGIO** or this sign.

- Be prepared to have to pay:
  per person
  for the car (if applicable)
  for the tent or caravan plot
  for electricity
  for hot showers
- You must provide proof of identity, such as your passport.
- You can obtain lists of campsites from local tourist offices [*see p. 24*] and from ENIT in London.
- To book plots in advance (particularly recommended in July and August) write to the **Centro Internazionale Prenotazioni Campeggio, Casella Postale 649, 1-50100 Firenze, Italy.**
- Some campsites offer discounts to campers with the International Camping Carnet.
- Camping off-site is allowed except in state forests and national parks. It is always best to ask permission from the landowner.

Youth hostels

- Look for the words:
  **OSTELLO PER LA
  GIOVENTÙ**, or this sign.
- You will be asked for a
  YHA card and your
  passport on arrival.
- Food and cooking facilities
  vary from hostel to hostel
  and you may have to help
  with domestic chores.
- You will have to hire sheets on arrival.
- In the high season it is advisable to book beds in advance, and your stay will be limited to a maximum of three consecutive nights per hostel.
- Apply to ENIT or local tourist offices in Italy [*see p. 24*] for lists of youth hostels and details of regulations for hostellers.
- For buying or replacing camping equipment, see p. 54.

WHAT TO SAY

I have a booking	**Ho una prenotazione**
	o oona prenotatzi-*oneh*
Have you any vacancies?	**Avete dei posti liberi?**
	avet-eh day postee *leeberee*
It's for ...	**È per ...**
	eh pair ...
one adult/one person	**un adulto/una persona**
	*oo*n ad*oo*lto/*oo*na pairs*o*na
two adults/two people	**due adulti/due persone**
	d*oo*eh ad*oo*ltee/d*oo*eh pairs*o*neh
and one child	**e un bambino**
	eh *oo*n bamb*ee*no
and two children	**e due bambini**
	eh d*oo*eh bamb*ee*nee
It's for ...	**È per ...**
	eh pair ...
one night	**una notte**
	*oo*na not-teh

two nights	due notti
	dooeh not-tee
one week	una settimana
	oona set-timan-ah
two weeks	due settimane
	dooeh set-timan-eh
How much is it ...	Quant'è ...
	quanteh ...
for the tent?	per la tenda?
	pair la tenda
for the caravan?	per la roulotte?
	pair la roolot
for the car?	per la macchina?
	pair la mac-keena
for the electricity?	per l'elettricità?
	pair lelet-treechita
per person?	per persona?
	pair pairsona
per day/night?	per giorno/notte?
	pair jorno/not-teh
May I look round?	Potrei dare uno sguardo?
	potray dar-eh oono zgoo-ardo
At what time do you lock up at night?	A che ora chiudete di sera?
	ah keh ora kee-oodet-eh dee seh-ra
Do you provide anything ...	È possibile ...
	eh posseebeeleh ...
to eat?	mangiare qui?
	manjar-eh quee
to drink?	bere qui?
	baireh quee
Do you have ...	Avete ...
	avet-eh ...
a bar?	un bar?
	oon bar
hot showers?	docce con acqua calda?
	dot-cheh con acqua calda
a kitchen?	una cucina?
	oona coocheena
a laundry?	una lavanderia?
	oona lavanderee-ah
a restaurant?	un ristorante?
	oon ristoranteh

Do you have ...	**Avete ...**
	avet-eh ...
a shop?	**un negozio?**
	oon negotzi-o
a swimming pool?	**una piscina?**
	oona pisheena

[*For food shopping see p. 61, and for eating and drinking out see p. 81.*]

Where are ...	**Dove sono ...**
	dov-eh sonno ...
the dustbins?	**le pattumiere?**
	leh pat-toomee-aireh
the showers?	**le docce?**
	leh dot-cheh
the toilets?	**i gabinetti?**
	ee gabinet-tee
At what time must one ...	**A che ora si deve ...**
	ah keh ora see dev-eh ...
go to bed?	**andare a dormire?**
	andar-eh ah dormeereh
get up?	**alzare?**
	altzar-eh
Please have you got ...	**Per favore avete ...**
	pair fav-oreh avet-eh ...
a broom?	**una scopa?**
	oona scop-ah
a corkscrew?	**un cavatappi?**
	oon cavatap-pee
a drying-up cloth?	**uno straccio per asciugare?**
	oono strat-cho pair ashoogar-eh
a fork?	**una forchetta?**
	oona forket-ta
a fridge?	**un frigorifero?**
	oon frigoreefero
a frying pan?	**una padella per friggere?**
	oona padel-la pair freed-jereh
an iron?	**un ferro da stiro?**
	oon ferro da steero
a knife?	**un coltello?**
	oon coltel-lo
a plate?	**un piatto?**
	oon pee-at-to

a saucepan?	**una pentola?**
	oona pentola
a teaspoon?	**un cucchiaino?**
	oon cooc-kee-ah-*eeno*
a tin opener?	**un apriscatole?**
	oon apreescat-oleh
any washing powder?	**della polvere per lavare?**
	del-la polvereh pair lavar-eh
any washing-up liquid?	**del liquido per lavare i piatti?**
	del liquido pair lavar-eh ee pee-*at*-tee
The bill, please	**Il conto, per favore**
	il conto pair fav-oreh

Problems

The toilet	**Il gabinetto**
	il gabinet-to
The shower	**La doccia**
	la dot-cha
The tap	**Il rubinetto**
	il roobinet-to
The razor point	**La spina per il rasoio**
	la speena pair il razoyo
The light	**La luce**
	la loocheh
... is not working	**... non funziona**
	... non foontzi-ona
My camping gas has run out	**La bombola del gas è finita**
	la bombola del gaz eh feeneeta

LIKELY REACTIONS

Have you an identity document?	**Ha un documento di riconoscimento?**
	ah oon docoomento dee riconosheemento
Your membership card, please	**La sua tessera, per favore**
	la soo-ah tes-saira pair fav-oreh
What's your name? [*see p. 15*]	**Come si chiama?**
	com-eh see kee-*am*-ah
Sorry, we're full	**Spiacente, siamo al completo**
	spee-achenteh see-*am*-o al complet-o

How many people is it for?	**Per quante persone?**
	pair qu*a*nteh pairs*o*neh
How many nights is it for?	**Per quante notti?**
	pair qu*a*nteh n*o*t-tee
It's (8,000) lira . . .	**Fa (ottomila) lire . . .**
	fa (*o*t-tomeela) l*e*ereh . . .
per day/per night	**al giorno/per notte**
	al j*o*rno/pair n*o*t-teh

[*For numbers see p. 128.*]

Rented accommodation: problem solving

ESSENTIAL INFORMATION

● If you are looking for accommodation to rent, look out for:

DA AFFITTARE/AFFITTANSI	(to let)
APPARTAMENTO/ALLOGGIO	(flat)
VILLA	(villa)
VILLETTA/VILLINO	(cottage)
CHALET	(chalet)

● For arranging details of your let, see 'Hotel', p. 26.
● Key words you will meet if renting on the spot:

il deposito	deposit
il dep*o*z-eeto	
le chiavi	keys
leh kee-*a*hvee	

● Having arranged your own accommodation and arrived with the key, check the obvious basics that you take for granted at home.

Electricity: Voltage? Razors and small appliances brought from home may need adjusting. You may need an adaptor.

Gas: Town gas or bottled gas? Butane gas must be kept indoors, propane gas must be kept outdoors.

Cooker: Don't be surprised to find:
the grill inside the oven, or no grill at all
a lid covering the rings which lifts up to form a 'splash-back'
a mixture of two gas rings and two electric rings.

Toilet: Mains drainage or septic tank? Don't flush disposable nappies or anything else down the toilet if you are on a septic tank.

Water: Find the stopcock. Check taps and plugs – they may not operate in the way you are used to. Check how to turn on (or light) the hot water.

Windows: Check the method of opening and closing windows and shutters.

Insects: Is an insecticide spray provided? If not, get one locally.

Equipment: See p. 54 for buying or replacing equipment.

● You will probably have an official agent, but be clear in your own mind who to contact in an emergency, even if it is only a neighbour in the first place.

WHAT TO SAY

My name is ...	**Mi chiamo ...**
	mee kee-*am*-o ...
I'm staying at ...	**Sono al ...**
	*so*nno al ...
They've cut off ...	**Hanno interrotto ...**
	*a*n-no interr*o*t-to ...
the electricity	**l'elettricità**
	lelet-treechi*ta*
the gas	**il gas**
	il gaz
the water	**l'acqua**
	*la*cqua
Is there ... in the area?	**C'è .. nella zona?**
	cheh ... nel-la d*zo*na
an electrician	**un elettricista**
	oon elet-treech*i*sta
a plumber	**un idraulico**
	oon idr*a*-oolico
a gas fitter	**un addetto al gas**
	oon ad-d*e*t-to al gaz
Where is ...	**Dov'è ...**
	dov-*e*h ...
the fuse box?	**la scatola dei fusibili?**
	la sc*a*t-ola day foo*zee*bilee
the stopcock?	**il rubinetto principale?**
	il roobin*e*t-to princheep*a*l-eh
the boiler?	**il bruciatore del riscaldamento?**
	il broo-cha-*to*reh del riscaldam*e*nto
the water heater?	**lo scalda-acqua?**
	lo scalda-*a*cqua

Is there ...	**C'è ...**
	cheh ...
town gas?	**il gas di città?**
	il gaz dee chit-*ta*
bottled gas?	**gas in bombola?**
	gaz in b*o*mbola
a septic tank?	**una fossa settica?**
	oona f*o*s-sa s*e*t-teeca
central heating?	**il riscaldamento centrale?**
	il riscaldam*e*nto chentr*a*l-eh
The cooker	**Il fornello**
	il forn*e*l-lo
The hair dryer	**L'asciugacapelli**
	lashoogacap*e*l-lee
The heating	**Il riscaldamento**
	il riscaldam*e*nto
The immersion heater	**Il boiler**
	il b*oi*lair
The iron	**Il ferro da stiro**
	il f*e*rro da st*ee*ro
The pilot light	**La fiammella spia**
	la fee-am-m*e*l-la sp*ee*-ah
The refrigerator	**Il frigorifero**
	il frigor*ee*fero
The telephone	**Il telefono**
	il tel*e*phono
The toilet	**Il gabinetto**
	il gabin*e*t-to
The washing machine	**La lavatrice**
	la lavatr*ee*cheh
The water heater	**Lo scalda-acqua**
	lo scalda-*a*cqua
... is not working	**... non funziona**
	... non foontzi-*o*na
Where can I get ...	**Dove posso trovare ...**
	d*o*v-eh p*o*s-so trov*a*r-eh ...
an adaptor for this?	**una spina per questo?**
	oona sp*ee*na pair qu*e*sto
a bottle of butane gas?	**una bombola di gas butano?**
	oona b*o*mbola dee gaz boot*a*n-o
a bottle of propane gas?	**una bombola di gas propano?**
	oona b*o*mbola dee gaz prop*a*n-o

a fuse?	**un fusibile?**
	oon foozeebeeleh
an insecticide spray?	**una bombola insetticida?**
	oona bombola inset-ticheeda
a light bulb?	**una lampadina?**
	oona lampadeena
The drain	**Lo scarico**
	lo scarico
The sink	**Il lavandino**
	il lavandeeno
The toilet	**Il gabinetto**
	il gabinet-to
... is blocked	**... è otturato**
	... eh ot-toorat-o
The gas is leaking	**Il gas perde**
	il gaz pairdeh
Can you mend it straightaway?	**Può ripararlo subito?**
	poo-oh riparar-lo soobeeto
When can you mend it?	**Quando potrà ripararlo?**
	quando potra riparar-lo
How much do I owe you?	**Quanto Le devo?**
	quanto leh dev-oh
When is the rubbish collected?	**Quando raccolgono i rifiuti?**
	quando rac-colgono ee ree-fewtee

LIKELY REACTIONS

What's your name?	**Come si chiama?**
	com-eh see kee-am-ah
What's your address?	**Il suo indirizzo?**
	il soo-o indeerit-tzo
There's a shop ...	**C'è un negozio ...**
	cheh oon negotzi-o ...
in town	**in città**
	in chit-ta
in the village	**in paese**
	in pa-aiz-eh
I can't come ...	**Non posso venire ...**
	non pos-so veneereh ...
today	**oggi**
	od-jee

this week	**questa settimana**
	questa set-tim*an*-ah
until Monday	**fino a lunedí**
	f*ee*no ah loon-ed*ee*
I can come ...	**Posso venire ...**
	p*o*s-so ven*ee*reh ...
on Tuesday	**martedí**
	mart-ed*ee*
when you want	**quando vuole**
	qu*a*ndo voo-*o*leh
Every day	**Ogni giorno**
	*o*n-yee j*o*rno
Every other day	**Un giorno sí e uno no**
	oon j*o*rno s*ee* eh *oo*no n*o*h
On Wednesdays	**Tutti i mercoledí**
	t*oo*t-tee ee maircol-ed*ee*

[*For days of the week see p. 132.*]

General shopping

The chemist's

**ESSENTIAL
INFORMATION**

- Look for the word
  FARMACIA (chemist's)
  or this sign.
- Medicines (drugs) are
  only available at a
  chemist's.
- Some non-drugs can be
  bought at a supermarket
  or department store.
- Try the chemist *before* going to a doctor: they are usually qualified
  to treat minor injuries.
- Chemists take it in turns to stay open all night and on Sundays.
  A notice on the door headed **FARMACIE DI TURNO** or
  SERVIZIO NOTTURNO gives details of opening times.
- Some toiletries can also be bought at a **PROFUMERIA**, but they
  will be more expensive.
- Finding a chemist, see p. 18.

WHAT TO SAY

I'd like ...	Vorrei ...
	vorr*ay* ..
some Alka Seltzer	**dell'Alka Seltzer**
	del-l*alka* s*eltzer*
some antiseptic	**dell'antisettico**
	del-l*antis*et-tico
some aspirin	**dell'aspirina**
	del-laspir*eena*
some bandage	**delle bende**
	del-leh b*endeh*
some cotton wool	**del cotone**
	del cot*oneh*
some eye drops	**del collirio**
	del col-l*ee*-reeo

I'd like ...	**Vorrei ...**
	vorr*ay* ...
some foot powder	**del talco per piedi**
	del t*a*lco pair pee-*eh*dee
some gauze dressing	**della garza**
	del-la g*a*rdza
some inhalant	**dell'inalante**
	del-linal*a*nteh
some insect repellent	**della crema anti-insetti**
	del-la cr*e*m-ah anti-ins*e*t-tee
some lip salve	**della crema per le labbra**
	del-la cr*e*m-ah pair leh l*a*b-bra
some nose drops	**delle gocce per il naso**
	del-leh g*o*t-cheh pair il n*a*z-o
some sticking plaster	**del cerotto**
	del chairot-to
some throat pastilles	**delle pastiglie per la gola**
	del-leh past*ee*l-yeh pair la g*o*la
some Vaseline	**della Vaselina**
	del-la vazel*ee*na
I'd like something for ...	**Vorrei qualcosa per ...**
	vorr*ay* qualc*o*za pair ...
bites	**morsicature**
	mor-seecat*oo*reh
burns	**bruciature**
	broo-chat*oo*reh
chilblains	**screpolature**
	screp-olat*oo*reh
a cold	**il raffreddore**
	il raf-fred-d*o*reh
constipation	**stitichezza**
	stitik*e*t-tza
a cough	**la tosse**
	la t*o*s-seh
diarrhoea	**diarrea**
	dee-arreh-ah
ear-ache	**mal d'orecchie**
	mal dorr*e*k-kee-*e*h
flu	**influenza**
	infl*u*entza
scalds	**scottature**
	scot-tat*oo*reh

sore gums	**mal di gengive**
	mal dee jenjeeveh
sprains	**distorsioni**
	distor-seeonee
stings	**punture**
	poontooreh
sunburn	**scottature da sole**
	scot-tatooreh da sol-eh
car (sea/air) sickness	**mal d'auto (di mare/d'aereo)**
	mal da-ooto (dee mareh/da-eh-reho)
I need ...	**Avrei bisogno di ...**
	avray beezon-yo dee ...
some baby food	**cibi per bambini**
	cheebee pair bambeenee
some contraceptives	**contraccettivi**
	contrat-chet-teevee
some deodorant	**deodorante**
	deh-odoranteh
some disposable nappies	**pannolini per bambini**
	pan-noleenee pair bambeenee
some hand cream	**crema per le mani**
	crem-ah pair leh man-ee
some lipstick	**un rossetto**
	oon ros-set-to
some make-up remover	**latte detergente**
	lat-teh detergenteh
some paper tissues	**fazzoletti di carta**
	fat-zolet-tee dee carta
some razor blades	**lamette per rasoio**
	lamet-teh pair razoyo
some safety pins	**spille di sicurezza**
	speel-leh dee sicooret-tza
some sanitary towels	**assorbenti igienici**
	as-sorbenti eejen-eechi
some shaving cream	**crema da barba**
	crem-ah da barba
some soap	**sapone**
	saponeh
some sun-tan lotion/oil	**crema/olio solare**
	crem-ah/olyo solar-eh
some talcum powder	**borotalco**
	borotalco

I need ...	Avrei bisogno di ...
	avray beezon-yo dee ...
some Tampax	Tampax
	tampax
some toilet paper	carta igienica
	carta eejen-eeca
some toothpaste	dentifricio
	denteefreecho

[*For other essential expressions see 'Shop talk' p. 57.*]

Holiday items

ESSENTIAL INFORMATION

- Places to shop at and signs to look for:

LIBRERIA-CARTOLERIA	(stationery)
TABACCHERIA	(tobacconist's)
ARTICOLI DA REGALO	(presents)
FOTO-OTTICO	(photographer–optician)
ARTICOLI FOTOGRAFICI	(photographical items)

- and the main department stores:
  UPIM
  STANDA
  RINASCENTE

WHAT TO SAY

Where can I buy ... ?	Dove posso comprare ... ?
	dov-eh pos-so comprar-eh ...
I'd like ...	Vorrei ...
	vorray ...
a bag	una borsa
	oona borsa
a beach ball	un pallone da spiaggia
	oon pal-loneh da speead-ja
a bucket	un secchiello
	oon sec-kee-ello

an English newspaper	**un giornale inglese**
	oon jornal-eh inglaizeh
some envelopes	**delle buste**
	del-leh boosteh
a guide book	**una guida**
	oona gweeda
a map (of the area)	**una piantina (della zona)**
	oona pee-anteena (del-la dzona)
some postcards	**delle cartoline**
	del-leh cartoleeneh
a spade	**una paletta**
	oona palet-ta
a straw hat	**un cappello di paglia**
	oon cap-pel-lo dee pal-ya
a suitcase	**una valigia**
	oona valee-ja
some sunglasses	**degii occhiali da sole**
	del-yee oc-kee-al-ee da soleh
a sunshade	**un parasole**
	oon parasoleh
an umbrella	**un ombrello**
	oon ombrel-lo
some writing paper	**della carta da lettere**
	del-la carta da let-tereh
I'd like ... [*show the camera*]	**Vorrei ...**
	vorray ...
a colour film	**una pellicola a colori**
	oona pel-leecola ah coloree
a black and white film	**una pellicola in bianco e nero**
	oona pel-leecola in bee-anco eh nairo
for prints	**per fotografie**
	pair fotografee-eh
for slides	**per diapositive**
	pair dee-apozeeteeveh
12 (24/36) exposures	**da dodici (ventiquattro/trentasei) pose**
	da dodeechee (venteecoo-at-tro/trentasay) pozeh
a standard 8 mm film	**un film da otto millimetri normale**
	oon feelm da ot-to meel-leemetree normal-eh

I'd like ... [*show the camera*]	**Vorrei ...**
	vorr*ay* ..
a super 8 film	**un film super otto**
	oon feelm s*oo*per *o*t-to
some flash bulbs	**delle lampadine per flash**
	del-leh lampad*ee*neh pair flash
This camera is broken	**Questa macchina fotografica è rotta**
	questa m*a*c-keena fotogr*a*feeca eh r*o*t-ta
The film is stuck	**Il film è bloccato**
	il feelm eh bloc-c*a*t-o
Please can you ...	**Per favore potrebbe ...**
	pair fav-*o*reh potr*e*b-beh ...
develop/print this?	**sviluppare/stampare questo?**
	zveeloop-p*a*r-eh/stamp*a*r-eh questo
load the camera?	**caricare il film?**
	ca-ree-c*a*r-eh il feelm

[*For other essential expressions see 'Shop talk', p. 57.*]

The tobacconist's

ESSENTIAL INFORMATION

- Tobacco is sold where you see this sign.
- See p. 18 to ask if there is one nearby.
- Tobacconists always sell postage stamps and salt.
- A tobacconist's is sometimes part of a café-bar, a paper shop (**CARTOLERIA**) or newsagent.

WHAT TO SAY

A packet of cigarettes ...	**Un pacchetto di sigarette ...**
	oon pac-*ket*-to dee sigaret-teh ...
with filters	**con filtro**
	con *fee*ltro
without filters	**senza filtro**
	*sent*za *fee*ltro
king size	**formato lungo**
	format-o *loo*ngo
menthol	**al mentolo**
	al men*to*lo
Those up there ...	**Quelle là sopra ...**
	quel-leh la *so*pra ...
on the right	**a destra**
	ah *des*tra
on the left	**a sinistra**
	ah sin*ees*tra

These [*point*]	**Queste** qu*e*steh
Cigarettes, please	**Sigarette, per favore** sigar*e*t-teh pair fav-*o*reh
100, 200, 300, two packets	**Cento, duecento, trecento, due pacchetti** ch*e*nto d*oo*eh-ch*e*nto treh-ch*e*nto d*oo*eh pac-k*e*t-tee
Have you got ...	**Avete ...** av*e*t-eh ...
English cigarettes?	**sigarette inglesi?** sigar*e*t-teh ingl*ai*zee
American cigarettes?	**sigarette americane?** sigar*e*t-teh americ*a*n-eh
English pipe tobacco?	**tabacco inglese da pipa?** tab*a*c-co ingl*ai*zeh da p*ee*pa
American pipe tobacco?	**tabacco americano da pipa?** tab*a*c-co americ*a*n-o da p*ee*pa
rolling tobacco?	**tabacco sciolto?** tab*a*c-co sh*o*lto
A packet of pipe tobacco	**Un pacchetto di tabacco da pipa** oon pac-k*e*t-to dee tab*a*c-co da p*ee*pa
That one up there ...	**Quello là sopra ...** qu*e*l-lo la s*o*pra ...
on the right	**a destra** ah d*e*stra
on the left	**a sinistra** ah sin*ee*stra
This one [*point*]	**Questo** qu*e*sto
A cigar, please	**Un sigaro, per favore** oon s*ee*garo pair fav-*o*reh
This one [*point*]	**Questo** qu*e*sto
Some cigars	**Dei sigari** day s*ee*garee
Those [*point*]	**Quelli** qu*e*l-lee
A box of matches	**Una scatola di cerini** oona sc*a*t-ola dee cher*ee*nee

A packet of pipe cleaners	Un pacchetto di filtri per pipa
	oon pac-ket-to dee filtree pair peepa
[*show lighter*]	
A packet of flints	Un pacchetto di pietrine
	oon pac-ket-to dee pee-etreeneh
Lighter fuel	Della benzina per accendino
	del-la bendzeena pair at-chendeeno
Lighter gas, please	Gas per accendino, per favore
	gaz pair at-chendeeno pair fav-oreh

[*For other essential expressions see 'Shop talk', p. 57.*]

Buying clothes

ESSENTIAL INFORMATION

- Look for:
  ABBIGLIAMENTO PER SIGNORA (women's clothes)
  ABBIGLIAMENTO DA UOMO (men's clothes)
  CALZATURE (shoes)
- Don't buy without being measured first or without trying things on.
- Don't rely on conversion charts of clothing sizes [see p. 142].
- If you are buying for someone else, take their measurements with you.
- The department stores **STANDA, UPIM** and **RINASCENTE** all sell clothes and shoes.

WHAT TO SAY

I'd like . . .	**Vorrei . . .**
	vor*ray* . . .
an anorak	**una giacca a vento**
	oona j*ac*-ca ah v*en*to
a belt	**una cintura**
	oona chint*oo*ra
a bikini	**un due pezzi**
	oon d*oo*eh pet-tzee
a bra	**un reggiseno**
	oon red-jee-s*eh*no
a cap (swimming)	**una cuffia (da bagno)**
	oona c*oo*f-fee-ah (da b*an*-yo)
a cap (skiing)	**un berretto (da sci)**
	oon berr*et*-to (da sh*ee*)
a cardigan	**un golf**
	oon golf
a coat	**un cappotto**
	oon cap-p*ot*-to
a dress	**un vestito**
	oon vest*ee*to
a hat	**un cappello**
	oon cap-p*el*-lo

a jacket	una giacca
	oona jac-ca
a jumper	una maglia
	oona mal-ya
a nightdress	una camicia da notte
	oona cameecha da not-teh
a pair of pyjamas	un pigiama
	oon pid-jam-ah
a V-neck pullover	un pullover
	oon pool-lovair
a raincoat	un impermeabile
	oon impermeh-ah-beeleh
a shirt	una camicia
	oona cameecha
a skirt	una gonna
	oona gon-na
a suit	un completo
	oon complet-o
a swimming costume	un costume da bagno
	oon costoomeh da banyo
a T-shirt	una maglietta di cotone
	oona mal-yet-ta dee cotoneh
I'd like a pair of ...	Vorrei un paio di ...
	vorray oon payo dee ...
briefs (women)	mutandine
	mootandeeneh
gloves	guanti
	gwantee
jeans	jeans
	jeens
shorts	pantaloni corti
	pantalon-ee cortee
socks (short/long)	calze (corte/lunghe)
	caltzeh (corteh/loong-geh)
stockings	calze di nylon
	caltzeh dee nylon
tights	collants
	col-lan
trousers	pantaloni
	pantalon-ee
underpants (men)	slip da uomo
	slip da womo

I'd like a pair of ...	**Vorrei un paio di ...**
	vorr*ay* oon p*a*yo dee ...
shoes	**scarpe**
	sc*a*rpeh
canvas shoes	**scarpe di tela**
	sc*a*rpeh dee t*e*h-la
sandals	**sandali**
	s*a*ndalee
beach shoes	**sandali da spiaggia**
	s*a*ndalee da spee-*a*d-ja
smart shoes	**scarpe eleganti**
	sc*a*rpeh eleg*a*ntee
boots	**stivali**
	stee-v*a*l-ee
moccasins	**mocassini**
	mocas-s*ee*nee
My size is ...	**Porto il numero ...**
[*For numbers see p. 128.*]	p*o*rto il n*oo*mero ...
Can you measure me, please?	**Può prendermi la misura, per favore?**
	poo-*o* pr*e*ndermi la meez*oo*ra pair fav-*o*reh
Can I try it on?	**Posso provare?**
	p*o*s-so prov*a*r-eh
It's for a present	**È per un regalo**
	eh pair oon reg*a*l-o
These are the measurements ...	**Queste sono le misure ...**
[*show written*]	qu*e*steh s*o*nno leh miz*oo*reh ...
bust	**petto**
	p*e*t-to
chest	**torace**
	tor*a*cheh
collar	**colletto**
	col-l*e*t-to
hip	**fianchi**
	fee-*a*nkee
leg	**gamba**
	g*a*mba
waist	**vita**
	v*e*eta

Have you got something ...	Avete qualcosa ...
	avet-eh qualcoza ...
in black?	in nero?
	in nairo
in white?	in bianco?
	in bee-anco
in grey?	in grigio?
	in greed-jo
in blue?	in blu?
	in bloo
in brown?	in marrone?
	in marroneh
in pink?	in rosa?
	in roza
in green?	in verde?
	in vairdeh
in red?	in rosso?
	in ros-so
in yellow?	in giallo?
	in jal-lo
in this colour? [point]	in questo colore?
	in questo coloreh
in cotton?	in cotone?
	in cotoneh
in denim?	in jeans?
	in jeens
in leather?	in pelle?
	in pel-leh
in nylon?	in nylon?
	in nylon
in suede?	in pelle scamosciata?
	in pel-leh scamoshat-ah
in wool?	in lana?
	in lan-ah
in this material? [point]	in questo tessuto?
	in questo tes-sooto

[For other essential expressions see 'Shop talk', p. 57.]

Replacing equipment

ESSENTIAL INFORMATION

- Look for these shops and signs:
  ELETTRICISTA   (electrical goods)
  FERRAMENTA
  ELETTRODOMESTICI   (hardware)
  ARTICOLI PER LA CASA
  DROGHERIA   (household cleaning materials)
- In a supermarket look for this display:
  ARTICOLI CASALINGHI
- To ask the way to the shop see p. 18.
- At a campsite try their shop first.

WHAT TO SAY

Have you got ...	Avete ...
	avet-eh ...
an adaptor ? [*show appliance*]	una spina a riduzione?
	oona speena ah ridootzioneh
a bottle of butane gas?	una bombola di gas butano?
	oona bombola dee gaz bootan-o
a bottle of propane gas?	una bombola di gas propano?
	oona bombola dee gaz propan-o
a bottle opener?	un apribottiglie?
	oon ap-reebot-teel-yeh
a corkscrew?	un cavatappi?
	oon cavat-tap-pee
any disinfectant?	del disinfettante?
	del disinfet-tanteh
any disposable cups?	dei bicchieri da buttare?
	day beec-kee-airee da boot-tar-eh
any disposable plates?	dei piatti da buttare?
	day pee-at-tee da boot-tar-eh
a drying-up cloth?	uno straccio per asciugare?
	oono strat-cho pair ashoogar-eh
any forks?	delle forchette?
	del-leh forket-teh

a fuse? [*show old one*]	**un fusibile?**
	oon foozeebeeleh
an insecticide spray?	**uno spray insetticida?**
	oono spra-ee inset-teecheeda
a paper kitchen roll?	**un rotolo di carta da cucina?**
	oon rotolo dee carta da coocheena
any knives?	**dei coltelli?**
	day coltel-lee
a light bulb? [*show old one*]	**una lampadina?**
	oona lampadeena
a plastic bucket?	**un secchio in plastica?**
	oon sec-keeo in plasteeca
a plastic can?	**un recipiente di plastica?**
	oon recheepee-enteh dee plastceca
a scouring pad?	**una paglietta abrasiva?**
	oona pal-yet-ta abraseeva
a spanner?	**una chiave inglese?**
	oona kee-ahveh inglaizeh
a sponge?	**una spugna?**
	oona spoon-ya
any string?	**del cordino?**
	del cordeeno
any tent pegs?	**dei picchetti da tenda?**
	day pic-ket-tee da tenda
a tin opener?	**un apriscatole?**
	oon apreescat-oleh
a torch?	**una torcia?**
	oona torcha
any torch batteries?	**delle pile?**
	del-leh peeleh
a universal plug (for the sink)?	**un tappo (per lavandino)?**
	oon tap-po (pair lavandeeno)
a washing line?	**una corda per stendere?**
	oona corda pair stendereh
any washing powder?	**della polvere da lavare?**
	del-la polvereh da lavar-eh
a washing-up brush?	**uno spazzolino per piatti?**
	oono spat-tzoleeno pair pee-at-tee
any washing-up liquid?	**del sapone liquido per piatti?**
	del saponeh liquido pair pee-at-tee

[*For other essential expressions see 'Shop talk', p. 57.*]

Shop talk

ESSENTIAL INFORMATION

- Know your coins and notes:
  coins: see illustration
  notes: L500, L1000, L2000, L5000, L10,000, L20,000, L50,000
- Know how to say the important weights and measures:

50 grams	**cinquanta grammi**
	chinqu*a*nta gr*a*m-mee
100 grams	**cento grammi**
	chento gr*a*m-mee
200 grams	**duecento grammi**
	doo*e*h-chento gr*a*m-mee
½ kilo	**mezzo chilo**
	m*e*d-dzo k*ee*lo
1 kilo	**un chilo**
	oon k*ee*lo
2 kilos	**due chili**
	doo*e*h k*ee*lee
½ litre	**mezzo litro**
	m*e*d-dzo l*ee*tro
1 litre	**un litro**
	oon l*ee*tro
2 litres	**due litri**
[*For numbers see p. 128.*]	doo*e*h leetree

- You may see the words **etto** (100 grams) or **all'etto** (per 100 grams) on price tickets. This is a colloquial expression for 100 grams.
- In small shops don't be surprised if customers, as well as the shop assistant, say 'hello' and 'good-bye' to you.

CUSTOMER

Hello ⎤	**Buon giorno**
Good morning ⎦	boo-*o*n i*o*rno
Good afternoon (after 3 p.m.)	**Buona sera**
	boo-*o*na s*e*h-ra
Good-bye	**A rivederla**
	ah reeveh-d*ai*rla
I'm just looking	**Guardo soltanto**
	gw*a*rdo soltanto

Excuse me	**Mi scusi**
	mee sc*oo*zee
How much is this/that?	**Quanto costa questo/quello?**
	qu*a*nto c*o*sta qu*e*sto/qwel-lo
What's that?	**Che cos' è quello?**
	keh coz-eh qu*e*l-lo
What are those?	**Che cosa sono quelli?**
	keh c*o*za s*o*nno qu*e*l-lee
Is there a discount?	**C'è uno sconto?**
	cheh oono sc*o*nto
I'd like that, please	**Vorrei quello, per favore**
	vorr*a*y qu*e*l-lo pair fav-*o*reh
Not that	**Non quello**
	non qu*e*l-lo
Like that	**Come quello**
	c*o*m-eh qu*e*l-lo
That's enough, thank you	**Basta cosí grazie**
	b*a*sta coz*ee* gr*a*tzee-eh
More, please	**Ancora, per favore**
	anc*o*ra pair fav-*o*reh
Less than that	**Meno di cosí**
	m*e*n-o dee coz*ee*
That's fine ⎤ OK ⎦	**Va bene**
	va b*e*n-eh
I won't take it, thank you	**Non lo prendo, grazie**
	non lo pr*e*ndo gr*a*tzee-eh
It's not right	**Non va bene**
	non va b*e*n-eh
Thank you very much	**Molte grazie**
	m*o*lteh gr*a*tzee-eh
Have you got something ...	**Avete qualcosa ...**
	av*e*teh qualc*o*za ...
better?	**di meglio?**
	dee m*e*l-yo
cheaper?	**di meno caro?**
	dee m*e*n-o c*a*r-o
different?	**di diverso?**
	dee deev*a*irso
larger?	**di piú grande?**
	dee pew gr*a*ndeh
smaller?	**di piú piccolo?**
	dee pew p*i*c-colo

At what time do you ...	A che ora ...
	ah keh *ora* ...
open?	aprite?
	ap*ree*teh
close?	chiudete?
	kewd*e*t-eh
Can I have a bag, please?	Posso avere una borsa, per favore?
	pos-so av*ai*reh *oo*na b*o*rsa pair fav-*o*reh
Can I have a receipt?	Posso avere la ricevuta?
	pos-so av*ai*reh la reechev*oo*ta
Do you take ...	Accettate ...
	at-chet-*tat*-eh ...
English/American money?	soldi inglesi/americani?
	s*o*ldee ingl*ai*zee/americ*a*n-ee
travellers' cheques?	travellers' cheques?
	travellairs sh*e*ck
credit cards?	carte di credito?
	c*a*rteh dee cred-*ee*to
I'd like ...	Vorrei ...
	vorr*ay* ...
one like that	uno di quelli
	*oo*no dec qu*e*l-lee
two like that	due di quelli
	d*oo*eh dee qu*e*l-lee

SHOP ASSISTANT

Can I help you?	È da servire?
	eh da sairv*ee*reh
What would you like?	Che cosa desidera?
	keh coza dez*ee*dera
Will that be all?	È tutto?
	eh t*oo*t-to
Is that all?	Basta così?
	b*a*sta coz*ee*
Anything else?	Nient'altro?
	nee-ent*a*ltro
Would you like it wrapped?	Glielo incarto?
	lee-*e*l-o inc*a*rto

Sorry, none left	**Mi dispiace non ne ho piú** mee dispi-*a*h-cheh non neh o pew
I haven't got any	**Non ne abbiamo** non neh ab-bee-*a*m-o
I haven't got any more	**Non ne abbiamo piú** non neh ab-bee-*a*m-o pew
How many do you want?	**Quanti ne desidera?** quantee neh dez*ee*dera
How much do you want?	**Quanto ne vuole?** quanto neh vw*o*leh
Is that enough?	**È abbastanza?** eh ab-bast*a*ntza

Shopping for food

Bread

ESSENTIAL INFORMATION

- Finding a baker's, see p. 18.
- Key words to look for:
  PANETTERIA (baker's)
  PANIFICIO (baker's bread usually baked on premises)
  PANETTIERE (baker)
  PANE (bread)
- Supermarkets of any size nearly always sell bread.
- Opening times vary slightly from place to place but are generally 9–1 and 3.30–8. Most bakers open earlier than other shops and are closed one day a week – the day varies from town to town.
- Although large and small loaves can be bought, rolls are very popular and it is important to note that bread is usually bought by *weight*.
- Bakers often stock other groceries, particularly milk. There is no milk delivery service and the dairy (**LATTERIA**) is fast disappearing.

WHAT TO SAY

Some bread, please	**Del pane, per favore**
	del *pan*-eh pair fav-*oreh*
A loaf (like that)	**Una pagnotta (cosi)**
	oona pan-*yot*-ta (co*zee*)
A large one	**Una grande**
	oona *grandeh*
A small one	**Una piccola**
	oona *pic*-cola
A bread roll	**Un panino**
	oon pan*eeno*
250 grams of ...	**Duecentocinquanta grammi di ..**
	dooeh-chento-chinqu*anta* gram-mee dee ...

½ kilo of ...	**Mezzo chilo di ...**
	m*e*d-dzo k*ee*lo dee ...
1 kilo of ...	**Un chilo di ...**
	*oo*n k*ee*lo dee ...
bread	**pane**
	p*a*n-eh
white bread	**pane bianco**
	p*a*n-eh bee-*a*nco
wholemeal bread	**pane integrale**
	p*a*n-eh integr*a*l-eh
bread rolls	**panini**
	pan*ee*nee
crispy bread sticks	**grissini**
	gris-s*ee*nee
Two loaves	**Due pagnotte**
	d*oo*eh pan-y*o*t-teh
Four bread rolls	**Quattro panini**
	qu*a*t-tro pan*ee*nee

[*For other essential expressions see 'Shop talk', p. 57.*]

Cakes

ESSENTIAL INFORMATION

- Key words to look for:
PASTICCERIA	(cake shop)
PASTICCIERE	(pastry maker)
PASTE/DOLCI	(cakes, pastries, sweets)
- To find a cake shop, see p. 19.
- BAR-PASTICCERIA: a place to buy cakes and have a drink. Italians often go to a bar for a snack mid-morning as they eat very little for breakfast.
- Most bars only have a few tables and charge more for waiter service. See p. 81, 'Ordering a drink'.

WHAT TO SAY

The type of cakes in the shops varies from region to region, but it is usual to find a variety of biscuits and small cream-filled pastries called paste fresche. These are bought by weight and it is best to point to the selection you prefer.

100 grams of ...	**Cento grammi di ...**
	chento gram-mee dee ...
200 grams of ...	**Duecento grammi di ..**
	dooeh-chento gram-mee dee ...
½ kilo of ...	**Mezzo chilo di ...**
	med-dzo keelo dee ...
cream pastries	**paste fresche**
	pasteh freskeh
biscuits	**biscotti**
	biscot-tee
A selection, please	**Misto, per favore**
	meesto pair fav-oreh

You may want to buy larger pastries and cakes individually:

A cake (like that), please	**Una torta (cosi), per favore**
	oona tor-ta cozee pair fav-oreh
An (apple) tart	**Una crostata (di mele)**
	oona crostat-a dee mele
A doughnut	**Un bombolone**
	oon bomboloneh
A brioche	**Una brioche**
	oona bree-osh

[*For other essential expressions see 'Shop talk', p. 57.*]

Ice-cream and sweets

ESSENTIAL INFORMATION

- Key words to look for:
GELATI	(ice-creams)
GELATERIA ⎤ **CREMERIA** ⎦	(ice-cream parlour)
PASTICCERIA	(cake shop)

- If you see a sign with **GELATI-PRODUZIONE PROPRIA**, this means that the ice-creams are made daily on the premises and are particularly good.

- Best known ice-cream brand-names are:

ALEMAGNA	**CHIAVACCI**
ALGIDA	**MOTTA**
BESANA	**SAMMONTANA**

- Every **gelateria** and **cremeria** has its own specialities which will either be described on menu cards or displayed on posters. Specialities vary from region to region.

- Pre-packed sweets are also available in supermarkets, bars and bakers' shops.

WHAT TO SAY

A . . . ice, please	**Per favore, un gelato . . .**
	pair fav-oreh oon jelat-o . . .
chocolate	**al cioccolato**
	al choc-colat-o
lemon	**al limone**
	al leemoneh
nougat	**al torroncino**
	al torroncheeno
peach	**alla pesca**
	al-la pesca
pistachio	**al pistacchio**
	al peestac-keeo
strawberry	**alla fragola**
	al-la fragola
vanilla	**alla crema**
	al-la crem-ah

(1,000) lira's worth	**Da (mille) lire**
	da (meeleh) leereh
A single cone [*specify flavour, as above*]	**Un cono**
	oon cono
Two singles	**Due coni**
	dooeh conee
A double cone	**Un cono a due gusti**
	oon cono ah dooeh goostee
Two doubles	**Due coni a due gusti**
	dooeh conee ah dooeh goostee
A mixed cone	**Un cono misto**
	oon cono meesto
A tub	**Una coppa**
	oona cop-pa
A lollipop	**Un ghiacciolo**
	oon ghee-at-cholo
A packet of ...	**Un pacchetto di ...**
	oon pac-ket-to dee ...
100 grams of ...	**Cento grammi di ...**
	chento gram-mee dee ...
200 grams of ...	**Duecento grammi di ...**
	dooeh-chento gram-mee dee ...
chewing gum	**cicles**
	cheec-lez
chocolates	**cioccolatini**
	choc-colat-eenee
mints	**caramelle alla menta**
	caramel-leh al-la menta
sweets	**caramelle**
	caramel-leh
toffees	**caramelle mu**
	caramel-leh moo

[*For other essential expressions see* 'Shop talk', *p. 57.*]

In the supermarket

ESSENTIAL INFORMATION

- The place to ask for: [see p. 18]

SUPERMERCATO	(supermarket)
SUPERMERCATO-ALIMENTARI	(food supermarket)

- Supermarket chains which can be found in most parts of Italy:

COOP	STANDA
PAM	UPIM
GAROSCI	

- Key instructions on signs in the shop:

ENTRATA	(entrance)
USCITA	(exit)
VIETATO L'INGRESSO	(no entry)
CASSA	(cash desk, check-out)
OFFERTA SPECIALE	(special offer)
CARRELLI	(trolleys)

- Opening times vary but are generally 9–12.30 and 3.30–7.30.
- For non-food items see 'Replacing equipment', p. 54.
- No need to say anything in a supermarket, but ask if you can't see what you want.

WHAT TO SAY

Excuse me, please	**Mi scusi, per favore**
	mee sc*oo*zee pair fav-*o*reh
Where is ...	**Dov'è ...**
	dov-*eh* ...
the bread?	**il pane?**
	il p*a*n-eh
the butter?	**il burro?**
	il b*oo*rro
the cheese?	**il formaggio?**
	il form*a*d-jo
the chocolate?	**il cioccolato?**
	il choc-col*a*t-o
the coffee?	**il caffè?**
	il caf-f*e*h
the cooking oil?	**l'olio per friggere?**
	l*o*l-yo pair fr*i*d-jereh

the fresh fish?	**il pesce fresco**
	il pesheh fresco
the fruit?	**la frutta?**
	la froot-ta
the jam?	**la marmellata?**
	la marmel-lat-ah
the meat?	**la carne?**
	la carneh
the milk?	**il latte?**
	il lat-teh
the mineral water?	**l'acqua minerale?**
	lacqua mineral-eh
the salt?	**il sale?**
	il sal-eh
the sugar?	**lo zucchero?**
	lo dzooc-kero
the tea?	**il tè?**
	il teh
the tinned fish?	**il pesce in scatola?**
	il pesheh in scat-ola
the tinned fruit?	**la frutta sciroppata?**
	la froot-ta sheerop-pat-ah
the vinegar?	**l'aceto?**
	lacheh-to
the wine?	**il vino?**
	il veeno
the yogurt?	**lo yogurt?**
	lo yogurt
the pasta?	**la pasta?**
	la pasta
the vegetable section?	**il reparto verdura?**
	il reparto vairdoo-ra
Where are ...	**Dove sono ...**
	dov-eh sonno ...
the biscuits?	**i biscotti?**
	ee beescot-tee
the crisps?	**le patatine fritte?**
	leh patateeneh freet-teh
the eggs?	**le uova?**
	leh wova
the frozen foods?	**i surgelati?**
	ee soor-jelat-ee

Where are ...	Dove sono ...
	dov-eh sonno ...
the fruit juices?	i succhi di frutta?
	ee sooc-kee dee froot-ta
the seafoods?	i frutti di mare?
	ee froot-tee dee mar-eh
the soft drinks?	le analcoliche?
	leh an-alcol-eekeh
the sweets?	i dolci?
	ee dolchi
the tinned foods?	i cibi in scatola?
	ee cheebee in scat-ola

[*For other essential expressions see 'Shop talk', p. 57.*]

Picnic food

ESSENTIAL INFORMATION

● Key words to look for:
  SALUMERIA
  SALUMI   ] (delicatessen)
  GASTRONOMIA
● In these shops you can buy a wide variety of food such as ham, salami, cheese, olives, appetizers, sausages, and freshly made take-away dishes. Specialities differ from region to region.
● Weight guide:
  4–6 oz/150 g of prepared salad per two people, if eaten as a starter to substantial meal.
  3–4 oz/100 g of prepared salad per person, if to be eaten as the main part of a picnic-type meal.

WHAT TO SAY

One slice of ...	Una fetta di ...
	oona fet-ta dee ...
Two slices of ...	Due fette di ...
	dooeh fet-teh dee ...
roast beef	arrosto
	arrosto

roast pork	**arrosto di maiale**
	arrosto dee mah-*yal*-eh
tongue	**lingua**
	l*i*n-gwa
veal with mayonnaise	**vitello tonnato**
	veet*e*l-lo ton-*nat*-o
bacon	**pancetta**
	panch*e*t-ta
salami (raw/cooked)	**salame (crudo/cotto)**
	salam-eh (cr*oo*do/c*o*t-to)
ham (raw/cooked)	**prosciutto (crudo/cotto)**
	prosh*oo*t-to (cr*oo*do/c*o*t-to)
meat loaf	**polpettone arrosto**
	polpet-toneh arr*o*sto
100 grams of ...	**Cento grammi di ...**
	ch*e*nto gr*a*m-mee dee ...
150 grams of ...	**Centocinquanta grammi di ...**
	chento-chin-qu*a*nta gr*a*m-mee dee ...
200 grams of ...	**Duecento grammi di ...**
	dooehch*e*nto gr*a*m-mee dee ...
300 grams of ...	**Trecento grammi di ...**
	treh-ch*e*nto gr*a*m-mee dee ...
Russian salad	**insalata russa**
	insal*a*t-ah r*oo*s-sa
seafood salad	**insalata di mare**
	insal*a*t-ah dee m*a*reh
tuna and olive salad	**insalata di tonno e olive**
	insal*a*t-ah dee ton-no eh ol*ee*veh
frankfurter salad	**insalata di würsteln**
	insal*a*t-ah dee w*oo*rsteln
prawn salad	**insalata di gamberetti**
	insal*a*t-ah dee gambair*e*t-*tee*
rice salad	**insalata di riso**
	insal*a*t-ah dee r*ee*zo

You might also like to try some of these:

olive verdi	green olives
ol*ee*veh *vair*dee	
olive nere	black olives
ol*ee*veh n*ai*reh	

olive nere al forno	baked black olives
oleeveh naireh al forno	
olive verdi ripiene	stuffed green olives
oleeveh vairdee rip-yen-eh	
funghetti sott'olio	mushrooms preserved in oil
foonghet-tee sot-tol-yo	
peperoni sott'olio	peppers preserved in oil
peperonee sot-tol-yo	
peperoni arrosto	roasted peppers
peperonee arrosto	
peperoni ripieni	stuffed peppers
peperonee rip-yen-ee	
pomodori ripieni	stuffed tomatoes
pomodoree rip-yen-ee	
cipolle ripiene	stuffed onions
chipol-leh rip-yen-eh	
melanzane in parmigiana	aubergines cooked in tomato
melandzan-eh in parmijan-ah	sauce and parmesan cheese
zucchini in carpione	courgettes cooked in oil and
zooc-keenee in carp-yoneh	vinegar, sage and garlic
zucchini ripieni	stuffed courgettes
zuc-keenee rip-yen-ee	
patatine fritte	crisps, freshly made daily
patateeneh freet-teh	
lasagne al forno	wide, flat noodles baked in a sauce
lazan-yeh al forno	of meat and bechamel
gnocchi alla romana	small, flat semolina 'dumplings'
n-yoc-kee al-la roman-ah	with butter and parmesan cheese
cannelloni ripieni	large tubular pasta stuffed with
can-nel-lonee rip-yen-ee	meat, or spinach and cheese
gnocchi alla fontina	potato 'dumplings' with melted
n-yoc-kee al-la fonteena	fontina cheese
torta di verdura	vegetable pie
torta dee vairdoo-ra	
torta pasqualina	spinach, eggs and herbs in a puff
torta pasqwaleena	pastry pie
parmigiano	parmesan, a hard, strong cheese
parmijan-o	used in cooking, usually grated
robiola	a mild fresh white cheese made
rob-yola	from ewe's milk
pecorino	a strong hard cheese, eaten fresh or
pecoreeno	grated when mature

ricotta	a soft white, very bland curd cheese
ricot-ta	made from ewe's milk
fontina	a rich Alpine cheese usually melted
fonteena	in cooking
provolone	a hard yellow cow's milk cheese
provoloneh	displayed hanging up
gorgonzola	a blue-veined cheese with a rich soft
gorgon-tzola	texture
mozzarella	a white flavourless curd cheese,
mot-tzar-el-la	should be eaten very fresh

[*For other essential expressions see 'Shop talk', p. 57*]

Fruit and vegetables

ESSENTIAL INFORMATION

● Key words to look for:

FRUTTA	(fruit)
VERDURA	(vegetables)
PRIMIZIE	(an indication of freshness)
ALIMENTARI	(grocer's and greengrocer's)
MERCATO	(market)

● If possible, buy fruit and vegetables in the market, where they are cheaper and fresher than in the shops. Open-air markets are held once or twice a week in most areas (or daily in large towns), usually in the mornings.

● It is customary for you to choose your own fruit and vegetables at the market (and in some shops) and for the stallholder to weigh them and price them. You must take your own shopping bag: paper and plastic bags are not normally provided.

● Weight guide: 1 kilo of potatoes is sufficient for six people for one meal.

WHAT TO SAY

½ kilo (1 lb) of ...	**Mezzo chilo di ...**
	med-dzo keelo dee ...
1 kilo of ...	**Un chilo di ...**
	oon keelo dee ...

2 kilos of ...	**Due chili di ...**
	dooeh keelee dee ...
apples	**mele**
	mel-eh
bananas	**banane**
	banan-eh
cherries	**ciliegie**
	chil-yeh-jeh
grapes (white/black)	**uva (bianca/nera)**
	oova (bee-anca/naira)
oranges	**arance**
	arancheh
pears	**pere**
	paireh
peaches	**pesche**
	peskeh
plums	**prugne**
	proon-yeh
strawberries	**fragole**
	fragoleh
A pineapple, please	**Un ananas, per favore**
	oon ananas pair fav-oreh
A grapefruit	**Un pompelmo**
	oon pompelmo
A melon	**Un melone**
	oon meloneh
A water melon	**Un'anguria**
	oon-angoo-ria
250 grams of ...	**Duecentocinquanta grammi di ...**
	dooeh-chento-chinquanta gram-mee dee ...
½ kilo of ...	**Mezzo chilo di ...**
	med-dzo keelo dee ...
1 kilo of ...	**Un chilo di ...**
	oon keelo dee ...
1½ kilos of ...	**Un chilo e mezzo di ...**
	oon keelo eh med-dzo dee ...
2 kilos of ...	**Due chili di ...**
	dooeh keelee dee ...
artichokes	**carciofi**
	carchof-ee

aubergines	**melanzane**
	melandz*an*-**eh**
carrots	**carote**
	car*o*t-eh
courgettes	**zucchini**
	tzooc-k*ee*nee
green beans	**fagiolini**
	fad-jol*ee*nee
leeks	**porri**
	p*o*rree
mushrooms	**funghi**
	f*oo*nghee
onions	**cipolle**
	chip*o*l-leh
peas	**piselli**
	peez*e*l-lee
peppers (green/red)	**peperoni (verdi/rossi)**
	peper*o*nee (v*air*dee/r*o*s-see)
potatoes	**patate**
	pat*a*t-eh
spinach	**spinaci**
	speen*a*chee
tomatoes	**pomodori**
	pomod*o*ree
A bunch of ...	**Un mazzetto di ...**
	oon mat-tz*e*t-to dee ...
parsley	**prezzemolo**
	pret-tz*e*m-olo
radishes	**rapanelli**
	rapan*e*l-lee
A head of garlic	**Una testa d'aglio**
	oona t*e*sta d*a*l-yo
Some lettuce	**Dell'insalata**
	del-linsal*a*t-ah
A cauliflower	**Un cavolfiore**
	oon cavol-fee*o*reh
A cabbage	**Un cavolo**
	oon c*a*volo
A stick of celery	**Un sedano**
	oon s*e*dan-o
A cucumber	**Un cetriolo**
	oon chetree-*o*lo

| Like that, please | **Come quello, per favore**
com-eh quel-lo pair fav-oreh |

These are some fruit and vegetables which may not be familiar:

cachi kak-ee	soft, sweet winter fruit, like a large tomato
nespole nespoleh	medlars: small, slightly sour fruit, orange colour, juicy
cardi cardee	cardoons: the top stalks of the thistle artichoke
finocchi feenoc-kee	fennels: crunchy vegetable with aniseed flavour
radicchio rosso radeec-kee ros-so	small-leafed red salad with a slightly bitter flavour

[*For other essential expressions see 'Shop talk', p. 57.*]

Meat

ESSENTIAL INFORMATION

- Key words to look for:
  MACELLAIO (butcher)
  MACELLERIA (butcher's)
- Butchers, especially in small towns and villages, often use a white sheet hung outside the shop as a sign.
- Weight guide: 4–6 oz/125–200 g of meat per person for one meal.
- The diagrams opposite are to help you make sense of labels on counters and supermarket displays, and decide which cut or joint to have. Translations do not help, and you don't need to say the Italian word involved.
- Mutton and lamb are only sold and eaten during the Easter period.

Beef Manzo

1 Stinco
2 Muscolo
3 Girello
4 Coscia, noce, rosa
5 Lombo, filetto
6 Costata
7 Guancia, testa
8 Collo
9 Polpa di spalla
10 Costato
11 Punta di petto
12 Pancia

Veal Vitello

1 Ossobuco
2 Cosciotto, magatello, noce
3 Codino
4 Lombata, nodini, costolette, scamone
5 Filetto
6 Copertina di spalla
7 Spalla, capello del prete, fusello
8 Testina
9 Collo
10 Fiocco di petto
11 Punta di petto
12 Pancetta

Pork Maiale

1 Testina
2 Coste, lombata, lonza, filetto
3 Spalla, prosciutto di spalla
4 Coscio, prosciutto di mezzo
5 Petto, pancetta
6 Cosciotto
7 Coscia, zampone
8 Piedino

Lamb, kid Agnello, Capretto

1 Testina, collo
2 Sella, costolette
3 Cosciotto
4 Spalla
5 Petto

WHAT TO SAY

For a joint, choose the type of meat and then say how many people it is for:

Some beef, please	**Del manzo, per favore**
	del man-zo pair fav-oreh
Some lamb	**Dell'agnello**
	del-lan-yel-lo
Some pork	**Del maiale**
	del mah-yal-eh
Some veal	**Del vitello**
	del veetel-lo
A joint ...	**Un arrosto ...**
	oon arrosto ...
for two people	**per due persone**
	pair dooeh pairsoneh
for four people	**per quattro persone**
	pair quat-tro pairsoneh
for six people	**per sei persone**
	pair say pairsoneh

For steak, liver or heart, use the same idea:

Some steak, please	**Della bistecca, per favore**
	del-la beestec-ca pair fav-oreh
Some liver	**Del fegato**
	del feh-gat-o
Some kidneys	**Dei rognoni**
	day ron-yonee
Some heart	**Del cuore**
	del cworeh
Some sausages	**Delle salsiccie**
	del-leh salseet-cheh
Some mince	**Della carne tritata**
	del-la carneh treetat-ah
for three people	**per tre persone**
	pair treh pairsoneh
for five people	**per cinque persone**
	pair chinqueh pairsoneh

For chops do it this way:

Two veal escalopes	**Due fettine di vitello**
	dooeh fet-*teeneh* dee veet*el*-lo
Three pork chops	**Tre braciole di maiale**
	treh brach*oleh* dee may*al*-eh
Four lamb chops	**Quattro costolette d'agnello**
	qu*at*-tro costol*et*-teh dan-y*el*-lo
Five beef chops	**Cinque fettine di manzo**
	ch*inqueh* fet-*teeneh* dee m*andzo*

You may also want:

A chicken	**Un pollo**
	oon p*ol*-lo
A rabbit	**Un coniglio**
	oon con*eel*-yo
A tongue	**Una lingua**
	oona l*eengwa*

Other essential expressions [*see also p. 57*]:

Please can you ...	**Per favore potrebbe ...**
	pair fav-*oreh* potr*eb*-beh ...
clean it?	**pulirlo?**
	pool*eerlo*
mince it?	**tritarlo?**
	treet*arlo*
dice it?	**tagliarlo a pezzetti?**
	tal-y*arlo* ah pet-*tzet*-tee
trim the fat?	**togliere il grasso?**
	t*ol*-yereh il gr*as*-so

Fish

ESSENTIAL INFORMATION

- The places to ask for are:
  PESCHERIA   (fish shop)
  MERCATO DEL PESCE (fish market)
- Another key word to look for is FRUTTI DI MARE (shellfish).
- Large supermarkets usually have a fresh fish stall.
- Weight guide: 8 oz/250 g minimum per person for one meal of
  fish bought on the bone, i.e.

½ kilo/500 grams	for 2 people
1 kilo	for 4 people
1½ kilos	for 6 people

WHAT TO SAY

Purchase large fish and small shellfish by the weight:

½ kilo of ...	Mezzo chilo di ... med-dzo keelo dee ...
1 kilo of ...	Un chilo di ... oon keelo dee ...
1½ kilos of ...	Un chilo e mezzo di ... oon keelo eh med-dzo dee ...
anchovies	acciughe at-choogeh
cod	merluzzo merloot-tzo
eel	anguilla angweel-la
mussels (*two names*)	muscoli/cozze moos-colee/cot-tzeh
octopus	polipo poleepo
oysters	ostriche ostreekeh
prawns	gamberi gamberee
red mullet	triglie treel-yeh

sardines	**sardine**
	sardeeneh
scampi	**scampi**
	scampee
shrimps	**gamberetti**
	gamberet-tee
small squid	**calamaretti**
	calamaret-tee
squid	**calamari**
	calama-ree

Some large fish can be purchased by the slice:

One slice of ...	**Una fetta di ...**
	oona fet-ta dee ...
Two slices of ...	**Due fette di ...**
	dooeh fet-teh dee ...
Six slices of ...	**Sei fette di ...**
	say fet-teh dee ...
dogfish	**palombo**
	palombo
cod	**merluzzo**
	merloot-tzo
swordfish	**pescespada**
	pesheh-spad-ah
fresh tuna	**tonno fresco**
	ton-no fresco

For some shellfish and 'frying pan' fish, specify the number you want:

A crab, please	**Un granchio, per favore**
	oon grankeeo pair fav-oreh
A lobster	**Un'aragosta**
	oonaragosta
A red mullet	**Una triglia**
	oona treel-ya
A cod	**Un merluzzo**
	oon merloot-tzo
A trout	**Una trota**
	oona trot-a
A sole	**Una sogliola**
	oona sol-yola

A dory [*expensive*]	**Un'orata**
	oonor*at*-ah
A bass [*expensive*]	**Un branzino**
	oon brandz*ee*no
A mullet	**Un cefalo**
	oon ch*e*falo

Other essential expressions [*see also p. 57*]:

Please can you ...	**Per favore potrebbe ...**
	pair fav-*o*reh potr*e*b-beh ...
take the heads off?	**tagliare le teste?**
	tal-y*ar*-eh leh t*e*steh
clean them?	**pulirli?**
	pool*ee*rlee
fillet them?	**tagliarli in filetti?**
	tal-y*ar*lee in fil*e*t-tee

Eating and drinking out

Ordering a drink

ESSENTIAL INFORMATION

- The places to ask for [see p. 18]:
  BAR
  BAR-PASTICCERIA   (drinks and cakes)
  CAFFÈ
  BIRRERIA   (beer and snacks)
- By law the price list of drinks (LISTINO PREZZI) must be displayed somewhere in the bar.
- There is waiter service in some cafés, but you can drink at the bar or counter if you wish (cheaper). In this case you should first pay at the cash desk (CASSA) and then take the receipt (scontrino) to the bar and give your order.
- Service is normally included in the bill (servizio compreso) but if not should be 10% to 15%.
- Bars and cafés serve both non-alcoholic and alcoholic drinks. There are no licensing hours, and children are allowed in.
- Italians drink a range of aperitifs (aperitivi) and digestives (digestivi). Their names vary from region to region. Most of the aperitifs are types of vermouth - red or white, sweet or dry – made by different firms such as Campari, Punt e Mes and Martini. The digestives can be made from almonds, fruit, or herbs and are often thick and syrupy.

WHAT TO SAY

I'll have . . . please	Prendo per favore . . .
	prendo pair fav-oreh . . .
a black coffee (small and strong)	un caffè
	oon caf-feh
a black coffee (less strong)	un caffè lungo
	oon caf-feh loong-go
a coffee with a dash of cream	un caffè macchiato
	oon caf-feh mac-kee-at-o
a milky coffee (breakfast)	un caffelatte
	oon caf-eh-lat-teh

I'll have . . . please	**Prendo, per favore . . .**
	prendo pair fav-*oreh* . . .
a frothy white coffee	**un capuccino**
	oon capooch*eeno*
a tea	**un tè**
	oon teh
with milk	**al latte**
	al *lat*-teh
with lemon	**al limone**
	al leem*oneh*
a glass of milk	**un bicchiere di latte**
	oon beec-kee-*air*eh dee *lat*-teh
a hot chocolate	**una cioccolata calda**
	oona choc-col*at*-ah c*al*da
a mineral water	**una minerale**
	oona miner*al*-eh
an iced coffee	**una granita di caffè**
	oona gran*eeta* dee caf-*feh*
a lemonade	**una limonata**
	oona leemon*at*-a
a fresh lemon juice	**una spremuta di limone**
	oona sprem*oota* dee leem*oneh*
a Coca Cola	**una Coca Cola**
	oona coca cola
an orangeade	**un'aranciata**
	oonaranch*at*-a
a fresh orange juice	**una spremuta d'arancia**
	oona sprem*oota* dar*ancha*
a fresh grapefruit juice	**una spremuta di pompelmo**
	oona sprem*oota* dee pomp*elmo*
a pineapple juice	**un succo di frutta all'ananas**
	oon s*ooc*-co dee fr*oot*-ta al-l*ananas*
a peach juice	**un succo di frutta alla pesca**
	oon s*ooc*-co dee fr*oot*-ta al-la p*esca*
a lager	**una birra**
	oona b*eerra*
a dark beer	**una birra scura**
	oona b*eerra* sc*oo*-ra
A glass of . . .	**Un bicchiere di . . .**
	oon beec-kee-*air*eh dee . . .
Two glasses of . . .	**Due bicchieri di . . .**
	dooeh beec-kee-*air*ee dee . . .

red wine	vino rosso
	veeno ros-so
white wine	vino bianco
	veeno bee-anco
rosé wine	rosé
	rozeh
dry	secco
	sec-co
sweet	dolce
	dolcheh
A bottle of ...	Una bottiglia di ...
	oona bot-teel-ya dee ...
sparkling wine	spumante
	spoomanteh
champagne	champagne
	shampan-yeh
A whisky	Un whisky
	oon wisky
with ice	con ghiaccio
	con ghee-at-cho
with water	con acqua
	con acqua
with soda	con seltz
	con seltz
A gin	Un gin
	oon jeen
and tonic	con tonico
	con ton-eeco
with lemon	con limone
	con leemoneh
A brandy	Un cognac
	oon con-yac

Other essential expressions:

Miss! [this does not sound abrupt in Italian]	Signorina!
	seen-yoreena
Waiter!	Cameriere!
	cameree-aireh
The bill, please!	Il conto, per favore!
	il conto pair fav-oreh
How much does that come to?	Quanto fa?
	quanto fa

Is service included?	**Il servizio è compreso?**
	il sairv*i*tzio eh compra*i*zo
Where is the toilet, please?	**Dov'è il bagno per favore?**
	dov-*eh* il b*a*n-yo pair fav-*o*reh

Ordering a snack

ESSENTIAL INFORMATION

- Look for a café or bar with these signs:
  PANINI
  TRAMEZZINI ⎤
  TOASTS ⎦ (sandwiches)
  TAVOLA CALDA ⎤
  PIZZE
  PIZZERIA
  BIRRERIA ⎦ (hot snacks)
- In some regions mobile vans sell hot snacks.
- In bars, if you want to eat your snack at the counter you need to pay first at the cash desk and then hand the receipt to the waiter behind the bar.
- For cakes, see p. 62.
  For ice-cream, see p. 64.
  For picnic-type snacks, see p. 68.
  For ordering a drink, see p. 81.
- Small sandwiches called **tramezzini** are popular snacks and are made with a variety of fillings. It is best to point to the ones you fancy.
- If olives, anchovies, crisps and nuts are available in bars, their price will normally be included with the drinks.

WHAT TO SAY

I'll have . . . please	**Prendo, per favore . . .**
	pr*e*ndo pair fav-*o*reh . . .
a cheese roll	**un panino al formaggio**
	oon pan*ee*no al form*a*d-jo
a ham roll	**un panino al prosciutto**
	oon pan*ee*no al prosh*oo*t-to

I'll have . . . please	Prendo, per favore . . .
	prendo pair fav-*oreh* . . .
a salami roll	un panino al salame
	oon pan*ee*no al sal*a*m-eh
a sandwich (like that)	un tramezzino (così)
	oon tramed-dz*ee*no (co*zee*)
a pizza	una pizza
	oona p*ee*t-tza

These are some other snacks you may like to try:

una pizzetta al pomodoro	small tomato pizza, usually eaten
oona pit-*tzet*-ta al pomodoro	cold
una focaccia	a savoury bread. similar to pizza but
oona foc*at*-cha	without tomato spread
una focaccina al prosciutto	a ham sandwich made with focaccia
oona focat-ch*ee*na al	bread
prosh*oot*-to	
un toast (al prosciutto e	a toasted sandwich. normally made
formaggio)	with ham and cheese
oon tost (al prosh*oot*-to eh	
form*a*d-djo)	

[*For other essential expressions see 'Ordering a drink', p. 83.*]

In a restaurant

ESSENTIAL INFORMATION

- The place to ask for: **un ristorante** [*see p. 18*]
- You can eat at all these places:

RISTORANTE	
TRATTORIA	(cheaper)
ALBERGO	(hotel – often a fixed menu)
PENSIONE	(mainly residents – fixed menu)
ROSTICCERIA	
PIZZERIA	
BIRRERIA	(hot snacks)
TAVOLA CALDA	

- Menus are always displayed outside the larger restaurants and that is the *only* way to judge if a place is right for your needs.
- Some smaller restaurants do not have a written menu and you must ask the waiter what is available.
- Self-service restaurants are rare.
- Service (of 10% to 15%) is always included on the bill, but an extra tip is usually welcome.
- Restaurants are now obliged, by law, to give receipts, and you should insist on this.
- In the south of Italy the lunch break is longer than in the north, and dinner is eaten later in the evening.

WHAT TO SAY

May I book a table?	**Potrei prenotare un tavolo?**
	potray prenotar-eh oon tavolo
I've booked a table	**Ho prenotato un tavolo**
	o prenotat-o oon tavolo
A table ...	**Un tavolo ...**
	oon tavolo ...
for one	**per una persona**
	pair oona pairsona
for three	**per tre persone**
	pair treh pairsoneh
The à la carte menu, please	**Il menú alla carta, per favore**
	il menoo al-la carta pair fav-oreh

The fixed price menu	**Il menú a prezzo fisso** il men*oo* ah pr*e*t-tzo f*i*s-so
The (8,000) lira menu	**Il menú da (ottomila) lire** il men*oo* da (*o*t-tom*ee*la) l*e*ereh
The tourist menu	**Il menú turistico** il men*oo* toor*i*stico
Today's special menu	**I piatti del giorno** ee pee-*a*t-tee del j*o*rno
What's this, please? [*point to menu*]	**Che cos'è questo, per favore?** keh coz-*e*h questo pair fav-*o*reh
A carafe of wine, please	**Una caraffa di vino, per favore** oona car*a*f-fa dee v*ee*no pair fav-*o*reh
A quarter (25 cc)	**Un quarto** oon qu*a*arto
A half (50 cc)	**Un mezzo litro** oon med-dzo l*ee*tro
A glass	**Un bicchiere** oon beec- kee-*ai*reh
A bottle/a litre	**Una bottiglia/un litro** oona bot-t*ee*l-ya/oon l*ee*tro
A half-bottle	**Una mezza bottiglia** oona med-dza bot-t*ee*l-ya
Red/white/rosé/house wine	**Vino rosso/bianco/rosé/della casa** v*ee*no ros-so/bee-*a*nco/roz*e*h/ del-la c*a*za
Some more bread, please	**Ancora del pane, per favore** anc*o*ra del p*a*n-eh pair fav-*o*ren
Some more wine	**Ancora del vino** anc*o*ra del v*ee*no
Some oil	**Dell'olio** del-l*o*l-yo
Some vinegar	**Dell'aceto** del-lach*e*to
Some salt	**Del sale** del s*a*l-eh
Some pepper	**Del pepe** del p*e*h-peh
Some water	**Dell'acqua** del-l*a*cqua
With/without (garlic,	**Con/senza (aglio)** con/s*e*ntza *a*lye

How much does that come to?	**Quanto fa?**
	quanto fa
Is service included?	**Il servizio è compreso?**
	il sairvitzio eh compraiz-o
Where is the toilet, please?	**Dov'è il bagno, per favore?**
	dov-eh il ban-yo pair fav-oreh
Miss! [this does not sound abrupt in Italian]	**Signorina!**
	seen-yoreena
Waiter!	**Cameriere!**
	cameree-aireh
The bill, please	**Il conto, per favore**
	il conto pair fav-oreh
May I have a receipt?	**Potrei avere una ricevuta?**
	potray avaireh oona reechevoota

Key words for courses, as seen on some menus

[Only ask this question if you want the waiter to remind you of the choice.]

What have you got in the way of . . .	**Che cosa avete come . . .**
	keh coza avet-eh com-eh . . .
STARTERS?	**ANTIPASTI?**
	antipastee
SOUP?	**MINESTRE?**
	minestreh
EGG DISHES?	**UOVA?**
	wova
FISH?	**PESCE?**
	pesheh
MEAT?	**CARNE?**
	carneh
GAME?	**SELVAGGINA?**
	selvad-jeena
FOWL?	**POLLAME?**
	pol-lam-eh
VEGETABLES?	**CONTORNO?**
	contorno
CHEESE?	**FORMAGGI?**
	formad-jee
FRUIT?	**FRUTTA?**
	froot-ta
ICE-CREAM?	**GELATI?**
	jelat-ee

DESSERT?	DOLCI?
	dolchee

['*Pasta*', spaghetti, etc., are part of the MINESTRE course, see p. 93.]

UNDERSTANDING THE MENU

● You will find the names of the principal ingredients of most dishes on these pages:

Starters p. 68	Fruit p. 72
Meat p. 74	Cheese p. 70
Fish p. 78	Ice-cream p. 64
Vegetables p. 73	Dessert p. 62

Used together with the following lists of cooking and menu terms, they should help you to decode the menu.

● *Remember*, dishes vary considerably from region to region in Italy: a dish with the same name, e.g. gnocchi alla Romana (pasta 'dumplings' Roman style), might be cooked in a different way in Rome from Milan – or even from one restaurant to another in the same city. Also, the same dish might appear on menus all over Italy with a different name in each region! If in doubt, always ask the waiter.

● These cooking and menu terms are for understanding only – not for speaking.

Cooking and menu terms

affumicato	smoked
all'aglio e olio	with oil and garlic
agrodolce	sweet-sour
arrosto	roast
al basilico	with basil
ben cotto	well cooked
con besciamella	with bechamel sauce
in bianco	boiled, with no sauce
bollito	boiled/stewed
alla bolognese	Bologna style
brasato	cooked in wine
al burro	cooked in butter
alla cacciatora	cooked in tomato sauce
al cartoccio	baked wrapped in foil
alla casalinga	homely style
al civet	marinated and cooked in wine

cotto	cooked (as opposed to raw)
crudo	raw
al dente	not overcooked, firm texture
dorato	slightly fried (golden)
alle erbe	with herbs
da farsi	to be prepared
ai ferri	grilled without oil
alla fiorentina	Florentine style
alla fonduta	with fondue
al forno	baked
fritto	fried
in gelatina	in savoury jelly
grattuggiato	grated; baked in cheese sauce
alla griglia	grilled on the fire
imbottiti	stuffed
lesso	boiled
in maionese	in/with mayonnaise
alle mandorle	with almonds
alla marinara	with seafood
al marsala	with Marsala wine
alla milanese	fried in egg and breadcrumbs
alla napoletana	Neopolitan style
all'origano	with oregano (herb)
in padella	cooked and served in a frying pan
al pangrattato	with breadcrumbs
alla panna	cooked in cream
al parmigiano	with parmesan cheese
al pecorino	with pecorino cheese
al pesto	with basil and garlic sauce
alla pizzaiola	with tomato sauce and cheese
al prezzemolo	with parsley
ragù	rich tomato and meat sauce for pasta
alla ricotta	with ricotta cheese
ripieno	stuffed
alla romana	Roman style
al rosmarino	with rosemary
salsa	sauce
salsa verde	parsley and garlic sauce
in salmí	cooked in oil, vinegar and herbs
al sangue	rare (steak, etc.)
alla siciliana	Sicilian style

spiedini	skewers
allo spiedo	on the spit
stufato	stew
al sugo	cooked in sauce
trifolato	cooked with tomato and parsley
in umido	steamed; stewed
alla veneziana	Venetian style
alle vongole	with clam (shellfish) sauce
allo zabaglione	with eggs, sugar and Marsala wine
zuppa	soup

Further words to help you to understand the menu:

abbacchio	young spring lamb
amaretti	macaroons
anguilla	eel
animelle	sweetbreads
anitra	duck
baccalà	dried cod
bagna cauda	raw vegetables dipped in sauce of hot oil, garlic, anchovies and cream
bistecca alla fiorentina	T-bone steak
braciole	chops
brodo	broth
budino	like crème caramel; pudding
cacciagione	game
capperi	capers
capretto	kid
capriolo	deer
cassata	ice-cream cake with dried fruit
cervella	brains
cinghiale	boar
coppa	very lean bacon; cup (of ice-cream)
costate	large chops
costolette	small chops
cotechino	large pork sausage
crema	custard cream; cream soup
crostata	fruit or jam tart
crostini	small pieces of fried bread
fagiano	pheasant
fagioli	fresh or dried beans

fave	broad or butter beans
fegatini	chicken livers
fettine	small tender steaks
filetti	fillets
fragole di bosco	wild strawberries
frittata	omelette
frittelle	fritters
fritto misto	mixed fried meats
fritto di pesce	mixed fried fish
frutti di mare	shellfish
gelati	ice-cream
granita	water ice
grissini	crispy bread sticks
involtini	slices of meat, stuffed and rolled
lepre	hare
limone	lemon
lombata	sirloin
macedonia	fruit salad
mandorle	almonds
minestrone	vegetable soup
mortadella	large mild salami
ossibuchi	dish of shin of veal
pancetta	bacon
panna	cream
pasta asciutta	general name of cooked pasta
pasta frolla	rich shortcrust pastry
pasta sfogliata	puff pastry
peperonata	stew of green and red peppers
peperoncini	chili peppers
pernice	partridge
petti di pollo/tacchino	chicken/turkey breasts
piccata	small veal slices
pignoli	pine nuts
pinzimonio	raw vegetables to dip in oil
polpette	meatballs
prosciutto di Parma	raw ham from Parma
quaglia	quail
riso	rice
risotto	rice cooked in sauce
rolata	meat loaf stuffed with herbs
salame all'aglio	garlic sausage
salsiccia	sausage

saltimbocca alla romana	fried veal with ham and rosemary
scaloppine	small veal slices
semifreddo	ice-cream with biscuits
seppie	cuttle-fish
spezzatino	stew
stracciatella	hot broth with beaten egg
stracotto	beef stew with vegetables
tacchino	turkey
tartuffi	truffles
torta	cake
trippa	tripe
uccelli	small birds (e.g. thrushes)
uova	eggs
vongole	clams, cockles
zampone	pig's trotter stuffed with chopped, seasoned meat
zuppa inglese	chocolate trifle
zuppa pavese	broth, lightly boiled egg and cheese

Types of pasta

agnolini/agnolotti	like ravioli
cannelloni	large tubular pasta, often stuffed
cappelletti	stuffed pasta rings
conchiglie	shell-shaped pasta
ditali	short tubular pasta
farfalle	butterfly-shaped pasta
fettuccine	narrow ribbons of pasta
gnocchi	small potato or semolina 'dumplings'
lasagne	wide flat pasta
maccheroni	large spaghetti with hole in middle
pasta asciutta	general term for cooked pasta
pasta in brodo	small shapes of pasta in broth
pizza	flat 'bread' spread with tomato
polenta	porridge of maize flour
ravioli	stuffed square-shaped pasta
rigatoni	large-grooved tubular pasta
spaghetti	long, thin, round pasta
tagliatelle	narrow ribbon pasta
tortellini	stuffed pasta rings
vermicelli	very thin spaghetti, 'little worms'
ziti	tubular-shaped pasta

Health

ESSENTIAL INFORMATION

- For details of reciprocal health agreements between the UK and Italy, ask for leaflet SA 30 at your local Department of Health and Social Security a month before leaving, or ask your travel agent.
- In addition, it is preferable to purchase a medical insurance policy through the travel agent, a broker or a motoring organization.
- The Italian state medical insurance is called INAM.
- Take your own 'first line' first aid kit with you.
- For minor disorders and treatment at a chemist's see p. 41.
- For asking the way to a doctor, dentist, chemist's or Health and Social Security Office (for reimbursement) see p. 20.
- Once in Italy decide a definite plan of action in case of serious illness: communicate your problem to a near neighbour, the receptionist or someone you see regularly. You are then dependent on that person helping you obtain treatment.
- To find a doctor in an emergency look for:
  medici (in the Yellow Pages of the telephone directory)
  AMBULATORIO (surgery)
  PRONTO SOCCORSO (casualty department, first aid)
  H
  OSPEDALE] (hospital)
- Dial 113 for an emergency ambulance service.

What's the matter?

I have a pain in my ...	Mi fa male ... mee ·a mal-eh ...
ankle	la caviglia la caveel-ya
arm	il braccio il brat-cho
back	la schiena la skee-ehna
bladder	la vescica la vesheeca
bowels	l'intestino lintesteeno

breast	**il seno**
	il sen-o
chest	**il torace**
	il toracheh
ear	**l'orecchio**
	lorec-keeo
eye	**l'occhio**
	loc-yo
foot	**il piede**
	il pee-ehdeh
head	**la testa**
	la testa
heel	**il calcagno**
	il calcan-yo
jaw	**la mandibola**
	la mandeebola
kidney	**il rene**
	il reh-neh
leg	**la gamba**
	la gamba
lung	**il polmone**
	il polmoneh
neck	**il collo**
	il col-lo
penis	**il pene**
	il peh-neh
shoulder	**la spalla**
	la spal-la
stomach (abdomen)	**lo stomaco (addome)**
	lo stom-aco (ad-domeh)
testicle	**il testicolo**
	il testeecolo
throat	**la gola**
	la gola
vagina	**la vagina**
	la vajeena
wrist	**il polso**
	il polso
I have a pain here [*point*]	**Ho un dolore qui**
	o oon doloreh quee
I have toothache	**Ho male a un dente**
	o mal-eh ah oon denteh

I have broken …	**Ho rotto …**
	o rot-to …
my dentures	la dentiera
	la dentee-*ai*ra
my glasses	gli occhiali
	l-*yee* oc-kee-*a*l-ee
I have lost …	**Ho perso …**
	o p*ai*rso …
my contact lenses	le lenti a contatto
	leh l*e*ntee ah cont*a*t-to
a filling	un'otturazione
	oonot-too-ratzioneh
My child is ill	**Mio/a figlio/a è ammalato/a***
	mee-o/ah f*ee*l-yo/ah eh am-mal*a*t-o/ah
He/She has a pain in his/her …	**Ha un dolore …**
	ah oon dol*o*reh …
ankle [*see list above*]	alla caviglia
	al-la cav*ee*l-ya

How bad is it?

I'm ill	**Sto male**
	sto m*a*l-eh
It's urgent	**È urgente**
	eh oorjenteh
It's serious	**È grave**
	eh gr*a*v-eh
It's not serious	**Non è grave**
	non eh gr*a*v-eh
It hurts	**Fa male**
	fa m*a*l-eh
It hurts a lot	**Fa molto male**
	fa molto m*a*l-eh
It doesn't hurt much	**Non fa troppo male**
	non fa trop-po m*a*l-eh
The pain occurs …	**Il dolore si ripete …**
	il doloreh se*è* rip*e*t-eh …
every quarter of an hour	ogni quarto d'ora
	*o*n-yee qw*aa*rto d*o*ra

*For boys use 'o', for girls use 'a'.

every half-hour	**ogni mezz'ora**
	on-yee med-dzora
every hour	**ogni ora**
	on-yee ora
every day	**ogni giorno**
	on-yee jorno
most of the time	**quasi sempre**
	qua-zee sempreh
I've had it for ...	**L'ho da ...**
	lo da ...
one hour/one day	**un'ora/un giorno**
	oonora/oon jorno
two hours/two days	**due ore/due giorni**
	dooeh oreh/dooeh jornee
It's a ...	**È ...**
	eh ...
sharp pain	**un dolore acuto**
	oon doloreh acooto
dull ache	**un dolore sordo**
	oon doloreh sordo
nagging pain	**un dolore continuo**
	oon doloreh continoo-o
I feel ...	**Mi sento ...**
	mee sento ...
weak	**debole**
	deh-boleh
feverish	**la febbre**
	la feb-breh
I feel ...	**Ho ...**
	o ...
dizzy	**le vertigini**
	leh vairteejeenee
sick	**la nausea**
	la na-oozeh-ah

Already under treatment for something else?

I take ... regularly [*show*]	**Prendo regolarmente ...**
	prendo regolarmenteh ...
this medicine	**questa medicina**
	questa medicheena
these pills	**queste pillole**
	questeh peel-loleh

I have ...	**Ho ...**
	o ...
a heart condition	**mal di cuore**
	mal dee cworeh
haemorrhoids	**le emorroidi**
	leh em-orroydee
rheumatism	**i reumatismi**
	ee reh-oomatismee
I'm ...	**Sono ...**
	sonno ...
diabetic	**diabetico/a***
	dee-abet-eeco/a
asthmatic	**asmatico/a***
	azmat-eeco/a
pregnant	**incinta**
	eencheenta
allergic to (penicillin)	**allergico/a* alla (penicillina)**
	al-lairieeco/ah al-la (penicheel-leena)

Other essential expressions

Please can you help?	**Mi può aiutare per favore?**
	mee poo-o ayootar-eh pair fav-oreh
A doctor, please	**Un dottore, per favore**
	oon dot-toreh pair fav-oreh
A dentist	**Un dentista**
	oon denteesta
I don't speak Italian	**Non parlo italiano**
	non parlo italian-o
What time does ... arrive?	**A che ora arriva ...?**
	ah keh ora arreeva ...
the doctor	**il dottore**
	il dot-toreh
the dentist	**il dentista**
	il denteesta

*Men use 'o' women use 'a'.

From the doctor: key sentences to understand:

Take this ...	**Prenda questo ...**
	prenda questo ...
every day/hour	**ogni giorno/ora**
	on-yee jorno/ora
twice/four times a day	**due/quattro volte al giorno**
	dooeh/quat-tro volteh al jorno
Stay in bed	**Stia a letto**
	stee-ah ah let-to
Don't travel ...	**Non viaggi ...**
	non vee-ad-jee ...
for ... days/weeks	**per ... giorni/settimane**
	pair ... jornee/set-timan-eh
You must go to hospital	**Deve andare in ospedale**
	dev-eh andar-eh in osped-al-eh

Problems: complaints, loss, theft

ESSENTIAL INFORMATION

- Problems with:
  camping facilities, see p. 35
  household appliances, see p. 54
  health, see p. 94
  the car, see p. 108
- If the worst comes to the worst, find the police station. To ask the way. see p. 18.
- Look for:
  CARABINIERI ⎤
  POLIZIA ⎦ (police)
  VIGILI URBANI (traffic wardens)
  QUESTURA (police station)
- If you lose your passport go to the nearest British Consulate.
- In an emergency, dial 113 for fire and police.

COMPLAINTS

I bought this ...	Ho comprato questo ...
	o comprat-o questo ...
today	oggi
	od-jee
yesterday	ieri
	yeh-ree
on Monday [see p. 132]	lunedí
	loon-edee
It's no good	Non va bene
	non va ben-eh
Look	Guardi
	goo-ardee
Here [point]	Qui
	quee
Can you ...	Potrebbe ...
	potreb-be ...
change it?	cambiarlo?
	cambee-arlo
mend it?	aggiustarlo?
	ad-joostarlo
Here's the receipt	Ecco la ricevuta
	ec-co la reechevoota
Can I have a refund?	Mi può rimborsare?
	mee poo-o rimborsar-eh
Can I see the manager?	Posso vedere il direttore?
	pos-so ved-aireh il diret-toreh

LOSS
[See also 'Theft' below; the lists are interchangeable.]

I have lost ...	Ho perso ...
	o pairso ...
my bag	la borsa
	la borsa
my bracelet	il braccialetto
	il brat-chalet-to
my camera	la macchina fotografica
	la mac-keena fotograf-eeca
my car keys	le chiavi della macchina
	leh kee-ahv-ee del-la mac-keena

my car logbook	**il libretto della macchina**
	il libret-to del-la m*a*c-keena
my driving licence	**la patente**
	la pa*te*nteh
my insurance certificate	**il certificato**
	dell'assicurazione
	il chairtee-f*i*cat-o
	del-las-sicoo-ratzioneh
my jewellery	**i gioielli**
	ee joy*e*l-lee
everything!	**tutto!**
	t*oo*t-to

THEFT
[See also 'Loss' above; the lists are interchangeable.]

Someone has stolen . . .	**Qualcuno mi ha rubato . . .**
	qualc*oo*no mee ah roob*a*t-o . . .
my car	**la macchina**
	la m*a*c-keena
my car radio	**la radio della macchina**
	la r*a*d-yo del-la m*a*c-keena
my keys	**le chiavi**
	leh kee-*a*hv-ee
my money	**i soldi**
	ee s*o*ldee
my necklace	**la collana**
	la col-l*a*n-ah
my passport	**il passaporto**
	il pas-sap*o*rto
my radio	**la radio**
	la r*a*d-yo
my tickets	**i biglietti**
	ee beel-y*e*t-tee
my travellers' cheques	**i travellers cheques**
	ee travellairs sh*e*ck
my wallet	**il portafoglio**
	il portaf*o*l-yo
my watch	**l'orologio**
	lorol*o*djo
my luggage	**i bagagli**
	ee bag*a*l-yee

LIKELY REACTIONS: key words to understand

Wait	**Aspetti**
	asp*et*-tee
When?	**Quando?**
	qu*a*ndo
Where?	**Dove?**
	d*o*v-eh
Name?	**Il suo nome?**
	il soo-o n*o*m-eh
Address?	**L'indirizzo?**
	lindir*ee*t-tzo
I can't help you	**Non posso aiutarla**
	non pos-so ayoot*a*rla
Nothing to do with me	**Non posso farci nulla**
	non pos-so f*a*rchee n*oo*l-la

The post office

ESSENTIAL INFORMATION

- To find a post office, see p. 18.
- Key words to look for:
  POSTA
  POSTE E TELEGRAFI (PT)
  POSTE-TELECOMUNICAZIONI (PTT)
- It is best to buy stamps at the tobacconist's. Only go to the post office for more complicated transactions, like telegrams.
- See p. 47 for sign indicating tobacconist's.
- Letter boxes are usually red.
- For poste restante you should show your passport at the counter marked **FERMO POSTA** in the main post office, and pay a small charge.

WHAT TO SAY

To England, please	**Per l'Inghilterra, per favore**
	pair ling-eelt*ai*rra pair fav-*o*reh

[*Hand letters, cards or parcels over the counter.*]

To Australia	**Per l'Australia**
	pair la-oostra**l**-ya
To the United States	**Per gli Stati Uniti**
	pair l-yee st*at*-ee oo*neetee*

[For other countries see p. 136.]

How much is ...	**Quanto costa spedire ...**
	qu*a*nto c*o*sta sped-*ee*reh ...
this parcel (to Canada)?	**questo pacco (in Canada)?**
	qu*e*sto p*a*c-co (in c*a*nada)
a letter (to Australia)?	**una lettera (in Australia)?**
	oona l*e*t-tera (in ah-oostr*a*l-ya)
a post card (to England)?	**una cartolina (in Inghilterra)?**
	oona cart*o*leena (in ing-eelt*ai*rra)
Air mail	**Via aerea**
	v*ee*-ah ah-*ai*reh-ah
Surface mail	**Via normale**
	v*ee*-ah norm*a*l-eh
One stamp, please	**Un francobollo, per favore**
	oon francob*o*l-lo pair fav-*o*reh
Two stamps	**Due francobolli**
	d*oo*eh francob*o*l-lee
One (220) lira stamp	**Un francobollo da (duecento-**
	venti) lire
	oon francob*o*l-lo da (d*oo*eh-ch*e*nto v*e*ntee) l*ee*reh
I'd like to send a telegram	**Vorrei spedire un telegramma**
	vorr*ay* sped-*ee*reh oon telegr*a*m-ma

Telephoning

ESSENTIAL INFORMATION

- Unless you read and speak Italian well, it's best not to make telephone calls by yourself. Go to the main post office and write the town and number you want on a piece of paper. Add **con preavviso** if you want a person-to-person call, or **spese a carico del ricevente** if you want to reverse the charges.
- Telephone boxes are grey or yellow. You will find public telephones in most bars; look for this sign.

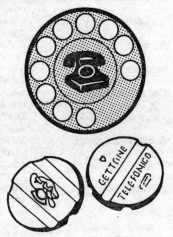

- To ask the way to a public telephone, see p. 21.
- To use a public telephone, you have to buy a special coin called a **GETTONE** (sold in bars, tobacconists post offices and some newsagents). For local calls (**CHIAMATE URBANE**), you must insert the gettone and wait for the dialling tone, before dialling.

  For longer distance calls (**CHIAMATE INTERURBANE**) at least six gettoni should be inserted before dialling.
- To call the UK using STD (**TELESELEZIONE**) dial the code 0044 then the number (less any initial O).
- For the USA you call the international operator (**ITALCABLE**), dial 170.

WHAT TO SAY

Where can I make a telephone call? **Dove posso fare una telefonata?**
dov-eh pos-so far-eh oona telefonat-ah

Local/abroad **Locale/all'estero**
local-eh/al-lestero

I'd like this number ... **Vorrei questo numero ...**
[show number] vorray questo noomero ...
in England **in Inghilterra**
in ing-eeltairra

in Canada **in Canada**
in canada

in the USA **negli Stati Uniti**
nel-yee stat-ee ooneetee

[For other countries see p. 136.]

Can you dial it for me, please? **Può farmi il numero, per favore?**
poo-o farmee il noomero pair fav-oreh

How much is it? **Quanto Le devo?**
quanto leh dev-o

Hello! **Pronto!**
pronto

May I speak to ... ? **Posso parlare con ... ?**
pos-so parlar-eh con

Extension ... **Interno ...**
intairno ...

I'm sorry, I don't speak Italian **Mi dispiace, non parlo italiano**
mee dispi-ah-cheh non parlo italian-o

Do you speak English? **Parla inglese?**
parla inglaizeh

Thank you, I'll phone back **Grazie, ritelefonerò**
gratzee-eh reetelefonero

Good-bye **A rivederci**
ah reevedairchee

LIKELY REACTIONS

That's (1,500) lira	**Fa (millecinquecento) lire** fa (meel-leh chinqueh-chento) leereh
Cabin number (3) [For numbers see p. 128.]	**Cabina numero (tre)** cabeena noomero (treh)
Don't hang up	**Attenda** at-tenda
I'm trying to connect you	**Cerco di collegarla** chairco dee col-legarla
You're through	**Parli pure** parlee poor-eh
There's a delay	**C'è un ritardo** cheh oon reetardo
I'll try again	**Proverò ancora** provero ancora

Changing cheques and money

ESSENTIAL INFORMATION

- Finding your way to a bank or exchange bureau, see p. 19.
- Look for these words on buildings:
  BANCA
  BANCO
  ISTITUTO BANCARIO } (bank)
  CASSA DI RISPARMIO
  CAMBIO-VALUTE (change bureau)
- To cash your normal cheques, exactly as at home use your banker's card where you see the Eurocheque sign. Write in English, in pounds.
- Exchange rate information might show the pound as:
  £, L, Lira Sterlina, L St, or even GB.
- Have your passport handy.

WHAT TO SAY

I'd like to cash ...	**Vorrei incassare ...** vorr*ay* incas-*sar*-eh ...
this travellers' cheque	**questo travellers cheque** questo travellairs sh*e*ck
these travellers' cheques	**questi travellers cheques** questee travellairs sh*e*ck
this cheque	**questo assegno** questo as-*se*n-yo
I'd like to change this into Italian lira	**Vorrei cambiare questi soldi in lire italiane** vorr*ay* cambi-*ar*-eh qu*e*stee s*o*ldee in l*ee*reh italian-eh
Here's ...	**Ecco ...** *e*c-co ...
my banker's card	**la mia carta assegni** la m*ee*-ah c*a*rta as-*se*n-ye
my passport	**il mio passaporto** il m*ee*-o pas-sap*o*rto

For excursions into neighbouring countries:

I'd like to change this ... [*show bank notes*] into Austrian schillings	**Vorrei cambiare questi soldi ...** vorr*ay* cambi-*ar*-eh qu*e*stee s*o*ldee... **in scellini austriaci** in shel-*lee*nee ah-oostr*ee*-achee
into French francs	**in franchi francesi** in fr*a*nkee franch*e*z-ee
into Italian lira	**in lire italiane** in l*ee*reh italian-eh
into Swiss francs	**in franchi svizzeri** in fr*a*nkee zv*ee*t-tzeree
What's the rate of exchange?	**Qual'è il cambio oggi?** qu*a*leh il c*a*mbeeo *o*d-jee

LIKELY REACTIONS

Passport, please	**Il passaporto, per favore** il pas-sap*o*rto pair fav-*o*reh
Sign here	**Firmi qui** f*ee*rmee qu*ee*

Your banker's card, please	**La sua carta assegni, per favore** la soo-ah carta as-sen-yee pair fav-oreh
Go to the cash desk	**Si accomodi alla cassa** see ac-comodee al-la cas-sa

Car travel

ESSENTIAL INFORMATION

- Finding a filling station or garage, see p. 21.
- Is it a self-service station? Look out for **SELF SERVICE.**
- Grades of petrol:
  BENZINA NORMALE (2 star, standard)
  BENZINA SUPER (3 star and above, premium)
  GASOLIO (diesel)
- 1 gallon is about 4½ litres (accurate enough up to 6 gallons).
- For car repairs, look for:
  AUTORIPARAZIONI (repairs)
  AUTORIMESSA (garage)
  MECCANICO (mechanic)
  ELETTRAUTO (for electrical faults)
  CARROZZERIA (for bodywork)
- Petrol stations are usually closed from 12 to 3, and very few offer a 24 hour service (except on motorways).
- In case of a breakdown or an emergency look for the **ACI** (Italian Automobile Club) sign, or dial 116 from any telephone box.
- Unfamiliar road signs and warnings, see p. 123.

WHAT TO SAY

[*For numbers see p. 128.*]

(Nine) litres of . . .	**(Nove) litri di . . .** (nov-eh) leetree dee . . .
(2000) lira of . . .	**(Duemila) lire di . . .** (dooeh meela) leereh dee . . .
standard/premium/diesel	**normale/super/gasolio** normal-eh/sooper/gazol-yo
Full, please	**Pieno, per favore** pee-ehno, pair fav-oreh

Will you check ... | **Può controllare ...**
poo-*o* control-l*a*r-eh ...

the oil? | **l'olio?**
l*o*l-yo

the battery? | **la batteria?**
la bat-ter*ee*-ah

the radiator? | **il radiatore?**
il rad-yat*o*reh

the tyres? | **le gomme?**
leh g*o*m-meh

I've run out of petrol | **Sono rimasta senza benzina**
s*o*nno reem*a*s-ta sentza bendz*ee*na

Can I borrow a can, please? | **Posso prendere a prestito
una latta, per favore?**
p*o*s-so prend*e*reh ah prest*ee*to
oona l*a*t-ta pair fav-*o*reh

My car has broken down | **La mia macchina s'è rotta**
la mee-ah m*a*c-keena seh r*o*t-ta

My car won't start | **La mia macchina non parte**
la mee-ah m*a*c-keena non p*a*rteh

I've had an accident | **Ho avuto un incidente**
o av*oo*to oon incheed*e*nteh

I've lost my car keys | **Ho perso le chiavi della macchina**
o p*a*irso leh kee-*a*h-vee del-la
m*a*c-keena

My car is ... | **La mia macchina è ...**
la mee-ah m*a*c-keena eh ...

two kilometres away | **a due chilometri**
ah d*oo*eh keel*o*metree

three kilometres away | **a tre chilometri**
ah treh keel*o*metree

Can you help me, please? | **Mi può aiutare, per favore?**
mee poo-*o* ayoot*a*r-eh pair
fav-*o*reh

Do you do repairs? | **Ripara le macchine?**
reep*a*r-ah leh m*a*c-keeneh

I have a puncture | **Ho una gomma a terra**
o oona g*o*m-ma ah t*e*rra

I have a broken windscreen | **Ho rotto il parabrezza**
o r*o*t-to il parabr*e*t-tza

I think the problem is here ... (*point*) | **Penso che il guasto sia qui ...**
p*e*nso keh il goo-*a*sto see-*a*h
quee ...

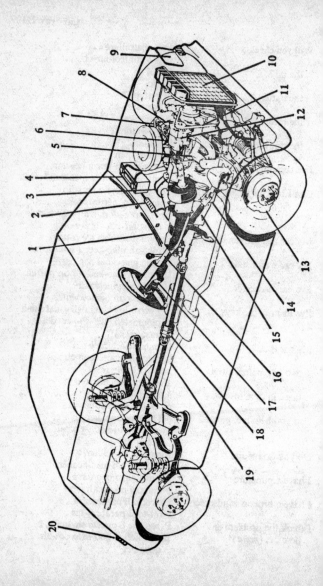

1 windscreen wipers	tergicristalli tairjee-crist*al*-lee	11 fan belt	cinghia del ventilatore chinghee-ah del ventilat-oreh
2 fuses	fusibili foozeebeelee	12 generator	dinamo d*ee*nam-o
3 heater	riscaldamento reescaldamento	13 brakes	freni frehnee
4 battery	batteria bat-t*eree*-ah	14 clutch	frizione freetzioneh
5 engine	motore motoreh	15 gear box	cambio cambeeo
6 fuel pump	pompa benzina pompa bendzeena	16 steering	sterzo stairtzo
7 starter motor	motorino d'avviamento motoreeno dav-vee-amento	17 ignition	accensione at-chensioneh
8 carburettor	carburatore carboorat-oreh	18 transmission	trasmissione trasmis-sioneh
9 lights	luci *loo*chee	19 exhaust	scappamento scap-pamento
10 radiator	radiatore rad-yat-oreh	20 indicators	lampeggiatori lampej-jat-oree

I don't know what's wrong	**Non so cosa non va** non so coza non va
Can you ...	**Può ...** poo-o ...
repair the fault?	**riparare il guasto?** reeparar-eh il goo-asto
come and look?	**venire a vedere?** veneereh a ved-aireh
estimate the cost?	**farmi un preventivo?** farmee oon preventeevo
write it down?	**scriverlo?** screeverlo
Do you accept these coupons?	**Accetta questi buoni?** at-chet-ta questee boo-onee
How long will the repair take?	**Quanto ci vorrà per ripararlo?** quanto chee vorra pair reeparar-lo
When will the car be ready?	**Quando sarà pronta la macchina?** quando sara pronta la mac-keena
Can I see the bill?	**Posso vedere il conto?** pos-so ved-aireh il conto
This is my insurance document	**Questa è l'assicurazione** questa eh las-sicooratzioneh

HIRING A CAR

Can I hire a car?	**Potrei noleggiare una macchina?** potray noled-jar-eh oona mac-keena
I need a car ...	**Ho bisogno di una macchina ...** o beeson-yo dee oona mac-keena ...
for two people	**per due persone** pair dooeh pairsoneh
for five people	**per cinque persone** pair chinqueh pairsoneh
for one day	**per un giorno** pair oon jorno
for five days	**per cinque giorni** pair chinqueh jornee
for a week	**per una settimana** pair oona set-timan-ah

Can you write down ...	**Può scrivermi ...**
	poo-*o* scr*ee*vermee ...
the deposit to pay?	**quant'è il deposito da pagare?**
	quant*eh* il dep*oz*-eeto da pag*ar*-eh
the charge per kilometre?	**quanto costa al chilometro?**
	qu*a*nto c*o*sta al keel*o*metro
the daily charge?	**quanto costa al giorno?**
	qu*a*nto c*o*sta al j*o*rno
the cost of insurance?	**il costo dell'assicurazione?**
	il c*o*sto del-las-sicoor*a*tzion*eh*
Can I leave it in (Turin)?	**Posso lasciarla a (Torino)?**
	p*o*s-so lash*a*rla ah (tor*ee*no)
What documents do I need?	**Quali documenti ci vogliono?**
	qu*a*l-ee docoom*e*ntee chee v*o*l-yono

LIKELY REACTIONS

I don't do repairs	**Non riparo auto**
	non reep*a*r-o *a*h-ooto
Where's your car?	**Dov'è la sua macchina?**
	dov-*e*h la s*oo*-ah m*a*c-keena
What make is it?	**Che tipo di macchina è?**
	keh t*ee*po dee m*a*c-keena eh
Come back tomorrow/on Monday	**Ritorni domani/lunedí**
	reet*o*rnee dom*a*n-ee/loon-ed*ee*

[*For days of the week see p. 132.*]

We don't hire cars	**Non noleggiamo macchine**
	non noled-j*a*mo m*a*c-keen*eh*
Your driving licence, please	**La patente, per favore**
	la pat*e*nteh, pair fav-*o*reh
The mileage is unlimited	**Il chilometraggio è illimitato**
	il keelometr*a*d-jo eh il-limit*a*t-o

Public transport

ESSENTIAL INFORMATION

- Finding the way to the bus station, a bus stop, a tram stop, the railway station and a taxi rank, see p. 18.
- Remember that queuing for buses is unheard of!
- Taxis can be found at taxi ranks in the main areas of a town, especially at the railway station.
- These are the different types of trains, graded according to speed (slowest to fastest):
  LOCALE
  DIRETTO
  ESPRESSO
  RAPIDO (sometimes first-class only, with supplement to be paid and seats to be reserved – especially on luxury high-speed trains)
- Key words on signs [see also p. 123]:

BIGLIETTI	(tickets)
BINARIO	(platform)
DEPOSITO BAGAGLI	(left luggage)
ENTRATA	(entrance)
FERMATA AUTOBUS	(bus stop)
FS, FERROVIE DELLO STATO	(Italian railways)
INFORMAZIONI	(information)
ORARIO	(timetable)
PROIBITO-VIETATO	(forbidden)
SALITA	(entrance for buses and tram)
USCITA	(exit)

- In the main cities automatic ticket systems are in operation on buses, trams and the underground. Tickets must then be bought in advance from bars and tobacconists. Ask for details at the local tourist information offices [see p. 24].

WHAT TO SAY

Where does the train for (Rome) leave from?	**Da dove parte il treno per (Roma)?** da dov-eh parteh il tren-o pair (roma)
At what time does the train leave for (Rome)?	**A che ora parte il treno per (Roma)?** ah keh ora parteh il tren-o pair (roma)
At what time does the train arrive in (Rome)?	**A che ora arriva il treno a (Roma)?** ah keh ora arreeva il tren-o ah (roma)
Is this the train for (Rome)?	**È questo il treno per (Roma)?** eh questo il tren-o pair (roma)
Where does the bus for (Florence) leave from?	**Da dove parte l'autobus per (Firenze)?** da dov-ch parteh la-ootoboos pair (feerentzeh)
At what time does the bus leave for (Florence)?	**A che ora parte l'autobus per (Firenze)?** ah keh ora parteh la-ootoboos pair (feerentzeh)
At what times does the bus arrive in (Florence)?	**A che ora arriva l'autobus a (Firenze)?** ah keh ora arreeva la-ootoboos ah (feerentzeh)
Is this the bus for (Florence)?	**È questo l'autobus per (Firenze)?** eh questo la-ootoboos pair (feerentzeh)
Do I have to change?	**Devo cambiare?** dev-o cambee-ar-eh
Where does ... leave from?	**Da dove parte ... ?** da doveh parteh ...
the bus	**l'autobus** la-ootoboos
the train	**il treno** il tren-o
the underground	**la metropolitana** la metropolitan-a

Where does . . . leave from?	**Da dove parte . . . ?**
	da doveh parteh . . .
the boat/ferry	**il vaporetto/il traghetto**
	il vap-oret-to/il trah-ghet-to
for the airport	**per l'aeroporto**
	pair la-airoporto
for the cathedral	**per la cattedrale**
	pair la cat-tedral-eh
for the beach	**per la spiaggia**
	pair la spee-ad-ja
for the market place	**per il mercato**
	pair il maircat-o
for the railway station	**per la stazione**
	pair la statzioneh
for the town centre	**per il centro città**
	pair il chentro chit-ta
for the town hall	**per il municipio**
	pair il moonicheepio
for St John's church	**per la chiesa di S. Giovanni**
	pair la kee-ehza dee san jovan-nee
for the swimming pool	**per la piscina**
	pair la pisheena
Is this . . .	**È questo . . .**
	eh questo . . .
the bus for the market place?	**l'autobus per il mercato?**
	la-ootobus pair il maircat-o
the tram for the station?	**il tram per la stazione?**
	il tram pair la statzioneh
Where can I get a taxi?	**Dove posso trovare un taxi?**
	dov-eh pos-so trovar-eh oon taxi
Can you put me off at the right stop, please?	**Può farmi scendere alla fermata giusta, per favore?**
	poo-o farmee shendereh al-la fairmat-ah joosta pair fav-oreh
Can I book a seat?	**Posso prenotare un posto?**
	pos-so prenotar-eh oon posto
A single	**Solo andata**
	solo andat-ah
A return	**Andata e ritorno**
	andat-ah eh reetorno
First class	**Prima classe**
	preema clas-seh

Second class	**Seconda classe**
	seconda clas-seh
One adult	**Un adulto**
	oon adoolto
Two adults	**Due adulti**
	dooeh adooltee
and one child	**e un bambino**
	eh oon bambeeno
and two children	**e due bambini**
	eh dooeh bambeenee
How much is it?	**Quanto costa?**
	quanto costa

LIKELY REACTIONS

Over there	**Di là**
	dee la
Here	**Qui**
	quee
Platform (1)	**Binario (uno)**
	beenar-eeo (oono)
At (four o'clock)	**Alle (quattro)**
	al-leh (quat-tro)
[For times see p. 130.]	
Change at (Milan)	**Cambi a (Milano)**
	cambee ah (meelan-o)
Change at (the town hall)	**Cambi al (municipio)**
	cambee al (moonicheepio)
This is your stop	**Questa è la sua fermata**
	questa eh la soo-ah fairmat-ah
There's only first class	**C'è solo la prima classe**
	cheh solo la preema clas-seh
There's a supplement	**C'è un supplemento**
	cheh oon soop-plemento

Leisure

ESSENTIAL INFORMATION

- Finding the way to a place of entertainment, see p. 18.
- For times of day, see p. 130.
- Important signs, see p. 123.
- In the more popular seaside resorts you have to pay to go on the beach and to hire deckchairs and sunshades.
- Smoking is forbidden in cinemas and theatres, unless specified.
- You should tip theatre usherettes.

WHAT TO SAY

At what time does . . . open?	**A che ora apre . . . ?**
	ah keh ora _a_preh . . .
the art gallery	**la galleria d'arte**
	la gal-ler_ee_-ah d_a_rteh
the botanical garden	**il giardino botanico**
	il jard_ee_no bot_a_n-eeco
the cinema	**il cinema**
	il ch_ee_nema
the concert hall	**l'auditorium**
	la-ooditor_ee_-oom
the disco	**la discoteca**
	la discotec-ah
the museum	**il museo**
	il mooz_ai_-o
the night club	**il night**
	il night
the sports stadium	**lo stadio**
	lo st_a_d-eeo
the swimming pool	**la piscina**
	la pish_ee_na
the theatre	**il teatro**
	il teh-_a_tro
the zoo	**lo zoo**
	lo dz_o_r
At what time does . . . close?	**A che ora chiude . . . ?**
	ah keh ora kee-_oo_deh . . .

the art gallery	**la galleria d'arte** la gal-ler*ee*-ah d*a*rteh

[see above list]

At what time does . . . start?	**A che ora inizia . . .?** ah keh ora een*ee*tzia . . .
the cabaret	**il cabaret** il cabar*e*h
the concert	**il concerto** il conch*a*irto
the film	**il film** il f*ee*lm
the match	**l'incontro** leenc*o*ntro
the play	**la commedia** la com-m*e*h-dia
the race	**la gara** la g*a*r-ah
How much is it . . .	**Quanto costa . . .** qu*a*nto c*o*sta . . .
for an adult?	**per un adulto?** pair oon ad*oo*lto
for a child?	**per un bambino?** pair oon bamb*ee*no
Two adults, please	**Due adulti, per favore** d*oo*eh ad*oo*ltee pair fav-*o*reh
Three children, please	**Tre bambini, per favore** treh bamb*ee*nee pair fav-*o*reh

[state price, if there is a choice]

Stalls/circle	**Platea/galleria** plat*e*h-ah/gal-ler*ee*-ah
Do you have . . .	**Avete . . .** av*e*t-eh . . .
a programme?	**un programma?** oon progr*a*m-ma
a guide book?	**una guida?** oona goo-*ee*da
Where's the toilet, please?	**Dov'è il bagno, per favore?** dov-*e*h il ban-yo pair fav-*o*reh
Where's the cloakroom?	**Dov'è il guardaroba?** dov-*e*h il gwardar*o*ba

I would like lessons in . . .	**Vorrei delle lezioni . . .**
	vorr*ay* del-leh letz*ee*onee . . .
skiing	**di sci**
	dee sh*ee*
sailing	**di vela**
	dee v*eh*-la
water skiing	**di sci d'acqua**
	dee shee d*a*cqua
sub-aqua diving	**di nuoto sub**
	dee nw*o*to s*oo*b
Can I hire . . .	**Potrei noleggiare . . .**
	potr*ay* noled-j*a*r-eh . . .
some skis?	**degli sci?**
	del-yee sh*ee*
some ski-boots?	**degli scarponi da sci?**
	del-yee scarp*o*nee da sh*ee*
a boat?	**una barca?**
	oona b*a*rca
a fishing rod?	**una canna da pesca?**
	oona c*a*n-na da p*e*sca
a deck chair?	**una sedia a sdraio?**
	oona s*e*d-ee-ah ah zdr*a*-yo
a sun umbrella?	**un ombrellone?**
	oon ombrel-l*o*neh
the necessary equipment?	**l'equipaggiamento necessario?**
	lequeepad-jam*e*nto neches-s*a*r-eeo
How much is it . . .	**Quanto costa . . .**
	qu*a*nto c*o*sta . . .
per day/per hour?	**al giorno/all'ora?**
	al j*o*rno/al-l*o*ra
Do I need a licence?	**Devo avere un'autorizzazione?**
	d*e*v-o av*ai*reh oon
	ah-ootorit-tzat-zioneh

Asking if things are allowed

ESSENTIAL INFORMATION

- May one smoke here?
  May we smoke here?
  May I smoke here?
  Can one smoke here?
  Can we smoke here?
  Is it possible to smoke here?

  } **Si può fumare qui?**

- All these English variations can be expressed in *one* way in Italian. To save space, only the first English version (May one . . . ?) is shown below.

WHAT TO SAY

Excuse me, please	**Mi scusi, per favore** mee scoozee pair fav-oreh
May one . . .	**Si può . . .** see poo-o . . .
camp here?	**campeggiare qui?** camped-jar-eh quee
come in?	**entrare?** entrar-eh
dance here?	**ballare qui?** bal-lar-eh quee
fish here?	**pescare qui?** pescar-eh quee
get a drink here?	**avere qualcosa da bere qui?** avaireh qualcoza da baireh quee
get out this way?	**uscire di qui?** oosheereh dee quee
get something to eat here?	**mangiare qualcosa qui?** man-jar-eh qualcoza quee
leave one's things here?	**lasciare della roba qui?** lashar-eh del-la roba quee
look around?	**guardare in giro?** goo-ardar-eh in jeero
park here?	**parcheggiare qui?** parked-jar-eh quee

May one . . .	Si può . . .
	see poo-*o* . . .
picnic here?	**fare un picnic qui?**
	f*a*r-eh oon picn*i*c quee
sit here?	**sedere qui?**
	sed*ai*reh quee
smoke here?	**fumare qui?**
	foom*a*r-eh quee
swim here?	**nuotare qui?**
	nwot*a*r-eh quee
take photos here?	**prendere una foto qui?**
	pr*e*ndereh oona f*o*to quee
telephone here?	**telefonare qui?**
	telefon*a*r-eh quee
wait here?	**aspettare qui?**
	aspet-t*a*r-eh quee

LIKELY REACTIONS

Yes, certainly	**Sí, certo**
	see ch*ai*rto
Help yourself	**Si serva**
	see s*ai*rva
I think so	**Penso di sí**
	p*e*nso dee see
Of course	**Naturalmente**
	natooralmenteh
Yes, but be careful	**Sí, ma faccia attenzione**
	see ma f*a*t-cha at-tentzi*o*neh
No, certainly not	**Certamente no**
	ch*ai*rtamenteh n*o*h
I don't think so	**Credo di no**
	cr*e*d-o dee n*o*h
Not normally	**Normalmente no**
	normalmenteh n*o*h
Sorry	**Mi dispiace**
	mee dispi-*a*h-cheh

Reference

PUBLIC NOTICES

● Key words on signs for drivers, pedestrians, travellers, shoppers and overnight guests.

ACCENDERE I FARI	Lights on
ACQUA POTABILE	Drinking water
AFFITTANSI	To let
ALT	Halt
APERTO	Open
ARRIVI	Arrivals
ASCENSORE	Lift
ASPETTARE	Wait
ATTENTI AL CANE	Beware of the dog
ATTENZIONE	Look out, beware
AUTOCARRI	Lorries, heavy vehicles
AUTO LAVAGGIO	Car wash
AUTOSTRADA (A PAGAMENTO)	Motorway (with toll)
AVANTI	Go
BAGNO	WC, bathroom
BIGLIETTERIA (A TERRA)	Ticket office (not on the bus)
BIGLIETTI	Tickets
BINARIO	Platform
CADUTA MASSI	Falling stones
CALDO (C)	Hot (tap) (H)
CAMERE LIBERE	Rooms to let
CARABINIERI	Police
CASSA	Cash desk
CHIUSO	Closed
CHIUSO PER FERIE	Closed for holidays
CHIUSO PER TURNO	Closed on shift basis
CON PIOGGIA, GELO, NEVE	In rain, ice, snow, (slippery road)
DA AFFITTARE	To let
DEPOSITO BAGAGLI	Left luggage
DEVIAZIONE	Diversion
DISPORSI SU UNA FILA	Single lane traffic
DIVIETO	Forbidden

DIVIETO DI PESCA	Fishing forbidden
DIVIETO DI SOSTA	No parking
DIVIETO DI TRANSITO	No through road
DOCCIA	Shower
DOGANA	Customs
DOMANI	Tomorrow
ECCETTO (AUTOBUS)	Except (buses)
ENTRATA	Entrance
ENTRATA LIBERA	Entrance free
FINE AUTOSTRADA	End of motorway
FERMATA (A RICHIESTA)	(Request) stop
FREDDO (F)	Cold (tap) (C)
FUMATORI	Smokers
GABINETTO	WC
GRATUITO	Free
GUIDA	Guide
GUIDARE LENTAMENTE	Drive slowly
INCROCIO	Crossroads
INGRESSO (LIBERO)	Entrance (free)
INIZIO AUTOSTRADA	Beginning of motorway
I TRASGRESSORI SARANNO PUNITI	Trespassers will be prosecuted
LAVORI IN CORSO	Road works
LIBERO	Free
LIMITE DI VELOCITÀ	Speed limit
LISTINO PREZZI	Price list
METROPOLITANA	Underground
MONETA	Coins
NON POTABILE	Not for drinking
NON TOCCARE	Do not touch
OBBLIGATORIO L'USO DELLE CATENE	Snow chains obligatory
OCCUPATO	Engaged
OFFERTA SPECIALE	Special offer
OGGI	Today
PAGAMENTO	Payment
PARCHEGGIO	Parking
PARCHEGGIO LIMITATO	Restricted parking
PARTENZE	Departures
PASSAGGIO A LIVELLO	Level crossing
PEDAGGIO	Toll
PEDONI	Pedestrians

PERICOLO	Danger
PIANO (PRIMO, SECONDO, TERZO, TERRA, SEMINTERRATO)	Floor (first, second, third, ground, basement)
POLIZIA	Police
PORTINAIO	Caretaker
PRECEDENZA	Priority
PRECEDENZA ALLA DESTRA	Priority to the right
PRENOTAZIONI	Reservations
PRONTO SOCCORSO	First aid
RALLENTARE	Slow down
RISERVATO	Reserved
SALA D'ATTESA	Waiting room
SALDI	Sales
SCALA MOBILE	Escalator
SCUOLA	School
SENSO UNICO	One way (street)
SENSO VIETATO	No entry
SERVIZI	WC
SIGNORE	Ladies
SIGNORI	Gentlemen
SILENZIO	Silence
SOSTA AUTORIZZATA (DALLE . . .)	Parking allowed (certain times)
SOSTA VIETATA	No parking
SOTTOPASSAGGIO	Subway
SPINGERE	Push
STRADA CHIUSA	Road closed
STRADA GUASTA	Road up
STRADA PERICOLOSA	Dangerous road
STRADA RISTRETTA	Road narrows
SUONARE IL CAMPANELLO	Ring the bell
SUONARE IN PORTINERIA	Ring the caretaker
SVOLTA	Bend
TENERE LA DESTRA	Keep right
TIRARE	Pull
TOELETTA	WC
UFFICIO INFORMAZIONI	Information office
USCITA	Exit

USCITA AUTOSTRADA	Motorway exit
USCITA D'EMERGENZA	Emergency exit
VAGONE RISTORANTE	Dining car
VALANGHE	Avalanches
VICOLO CIECO	Cul-de-sac
VIETATO	Forbidden
VIETATO FUMARE	No smoking
VIETATO IL SORPASSO	No overtaking
VIETATO INTRODURRE CANI	No dogs allowed
VIETATO L'INGRESSO (VEICOLI)	No entry (for vehicles)
VIETATO IL TRANSITO	No through road
VIETATO TRANSITO AUTOCARRI	No through road for lorries
ZONA DISCO	Parking disc required
ZONA PEDONALE	Pedestrian area
ZONA SLAVINE	Avalanche area

ABBREVIATIONS

ACI	Automobile Club d'Italia	Italian Automobile Club
AGIP	Azienda Generale Italiana Petroli	chain of petrol stations
alb	albergo	hotel
alt	altezza	height
ANAS	Azienda Nazionale Autonoma delle Strade Statali	State Highway Authority
avv	avvocato	solicitor
CIT	Compagnia Italiana Turismo	Italian Travel Agency
cm	corrente mese	instant
CRI	Croce Rossa Italiana	Italian Red Cross
dc	dopo Cristo	after Christ (AD)
dott	dottore	doctor (medical and university graduate)
EA	Ente Autonomo	Authority
EI	Esercito Italiano	Italian Army
ENIT	Ente Nazionale Italiano Turismo	Italian State Tourist Authority
fatt	fattura	invoice

ferr	ferrovia	railway
FS	Ferrovie dello Stato	State Railways
GdF	Guardie di Finanza	customs officers
h	ora	hour
ht	ettogrammo	100 grams
ing	ingegnere	engineer
INAM	Istituto Nazionale Assicurazione Malattie	National (Medical) Insurance
IVA	Imposta Valore Aggiunto	VAT
L it	Lire Italiane	Italian lira
L st	Lire Sterline	£ Sterling
naz	nazionale	national
PP TT	Poste Telecomunicazioni	post office
PS	Pubblica Sicurezza	police
PT	Poste Telegrafi	post office
racc	raccomandata	registered letter
RAI	Radio Audizione Italiana	Italian Broadcasting Company
sig	signore	Mr
sigra	signora	Mrs
signa	signorina	Miss
SpA	Società per Azioni	Limited Company
succ	succursale	branch
tel	telefono	telephone
vle	viale	boulevard
VU	Vigile Urbano	traffic police

NUMBERS

Cardinal numbers

0	zero	dzairo
1	uno	oono
2	due	dooeh
3	tre	treh
4	quattro	quaat-tro
5	cinque	chinqueh
6	sei	say
7	sette	set-teh
8	otto	ot-to
9	nove	noveh
10	dieci	dee-echee
11	undici	oondeechee
12	dodici	dodeechee
13	tredici	trehdeechee
14	quattordici	quat-tordeechee
15	quindici	quindeechee
16	sedici	sehdeechee
17	diciassette	deechas-set-teh
18	diciotto	deechot-to
19	diciannove	deechan-noveh
20	venti	ventee
21	ventuno	ven-toono
22	ventidue	ventee-dooeh
23	ventitré	ventee-treh
24	ventiquattro	ventee-quat-tro
25	venticinque	ventee-chinqueh
26	ventisei	ventee-say
27	ventisette	ventee-set-teh
28	ventotto	ventot-to
29	ventinove	ventee-noveh
30	trenta	trenta

For numbers beyond 20 follow the pattern of venti: *keep the final vowel except with one and eight.*

31	trentuno	tren-toono
35	trentacinque	trenta-chinqueh
38	trentotto	trentot-to
40	quaranta	quaranta

41	quarantuno	quarant-oono
45	quarantacinque	quaranta-chinqueh
48	quarantotto	quarantot-to
50	cinquanta	chinquanta
55	cinquantacinque	chinquanta-chinqueh
60	sessanta	ses-santa
65	sessantacinque	ses-santa-chinqueh
70	settanta	set-tanta
80	ottanta	ot-tanta
90	novanta	novanta
100	cento	chento
101	centouno	chento-oono
102	centodue	chento-dooeh
125	centoventicinque	chentoventee-chinqueh
150	centocinquanta	chento-chin-quanta
175	centosettantacinque	chentoset-tanta-chinqueh
200	duecento	dooeh-chento
300	trecento	treh-chento
400	quattrocento	quat-tro-chento
500	cinquecento	chinqueh-chento
1000	mille	meel-leh
1500	millecinquecento	meel-leh-chinqueh-chento
2000	duemila	dooeh-meela
5000	cinquemila	chinqueh-meela
10,000	diecimila	dee-echee-meela
100,000	centomila	chento-meela
1,000,000	un milione	oon meel-yoneh

Ordinal numbers

1st	primo (1°)	preemo
2nd	secondo (2°)	secondo
3rd	terzo (3°)	tairtzo
4th	quarto (4°)	quarto
5th	quinto (5°)	queento
6th	sesto (6°)	sesto
7th	settimo (7°)	set-teemo
8th	ottavo (8°)	ot-tavo
9th	nono (9°)	no-no
10th	decimo (10°)	decheemo
11th	undicesimo (11°)	oondeecheh-zeemo
12th	dodicesimo (12°)	dodeecheh-zeemo

TIME

What time is it?	**Che ora è?** keh ora eh
It's one o'clock	**È l'una** eh loona
It's ...	**Sono ...** sonno ...
two o'clock	**le due** leh dooeh
three o'clock	**le tre** leh treh
four o'clock	**le quattro** leh quat-tro
in the morning	**di mattino** dee mat-teeno
in the afternoon	**di pomeriggio** dee pomaireed-jo
in the evening	**di sera** dee saira
in the night	**di notte** dee not-teh
It's ...	**È ...** eh ...
noon	**mezzogiorno** med-dzojorno
midnight	**mezzanotte** med-dzanot-teh
It's ...	**Sono ...** sonno ...
five past five	**le cinque e cinque** leh chinqueh eh chinqueh
ten past five	**le cinque e dieci** leh chinqueh eh dee-echee
a quarter past five	**le cinque e un quarto** leh chinqueh eh oon quaarto
twenty past five	**le cinque e venti** leh chinqueh eh ventee
twenty-five past five	**le cinque e venticinque** leh chinqueh eh ventee-chinqueh
half past five	**le cinque e mezza** leh chinqueh eh med-dza
twenty-five to six	**le sei meno venticinque** leh say men-o ventee-chinqueh

twenty to six	**le sei meno venti**
	leh say men-o ventee
a quarter to six	**le sei meno un quarto**
	leh say men-o oon quaarto
ten to six	**le sei meno dieci**
	leh say men-o dee-echee
five to six	**le sei meno cinque**
	leh say men-o chinqueh
At what time ... (does the train leave)?	**A che ora (parte il treno)?**
	ah keh ora parteh il tren-o
At ...	**Alle ...**
	al-leh ...
13.00	**tredici**
	treh-deechee
14.05	**quattordici e cinque**
	quat-tordeechee eh chinqueh
15.10	**quindici e dieci**
	quin-deechee eh dee-echee
16.15	**sedici e quindici**
	seh-deechee eh quin-deechee
17.20	**diciassette e venti**
	deechas-set-teh eh ventee
18.25	**diciotto e venticinque**
	deechot-to eh ventee-chinqueh
19.30	**diciannove e trenta**
	dichan-noveh eh trenta
20.35	**venti e trentacinque**
	ventee eh trenta-chinqueh
21.40	**ventuno e quaranta**
	vent-oono eh quaranta
22.45	**ventidue e quarantacinque**
	ventee-dooeh eh quaranta-chinqueh
23.50	**ventitrè e cinquanta**
	ventee-treh eh chinquanta
0.55	**zero e cinquantacinque**
	dzairo eh chinquanta-chinqueh
in ten minutes	**fra dieci minuti**
	fra dee-echee meenootee
in a quarter of an hour	**fra un quarto d'ora**
	fra oon quaarto dora
in half an hour	**fra mezz'ora**
	fra med-dzora
in three-quarters of an hour	**fra tre quarti d'ora**
	fra treh quaartee dora

DAYS

Monday	**lunedí**
	loon-ed*ee*
Tuesday	**martedí**
	mart-ed*ee*
Wednesday	**mercoledí**
	maircol-ed*ee*
Thursday	**giovedí**
	jov-ed*ee*
Friday	**venerdí**
	venaird*ee*
Saturday	**sabato**
	s*a*bato
Sunday	**domenica**
	domen-eeca
last Monday	**lunedí scorso**
	loon-ed*ee* sc*o*rso
next Tuesday	**martedí prossimo**
	mart-ed*ee* pros-seemo
on Wednesday	**mercoledí**
	maircol-ed*ee*
on Thursdays	**al giovedí**
	al jov-ed*ee*
until Friday	**fino a venerdí**
	f*ee*no ah venaird*ee*
before Saturday	**prima di sabato**
	pr*ee*ma dee s*a*bato
after Sunday	**dopo domenica**
	d*o*p-o domen-eeca
the day before yesterday	**l'altro ieri**
	l*a*ltro y*a*iree
two days ago	**due giorni fa**
	dooeh j*o*rnee f*a*
yesterday	**ieri**
	y*a*iree
yesterday morning	**ieri mattina**
	y*a*iree mat-t*ee*na
yesterday afternoon	**ieri pomeriggio**
	y*a*iree pomair*ee*d-jo
last night	**ieri sera**
	y*a*iree seh-ra

today	**oggi**
	*o*d-jee
this morning	**questa mattina**
	qu*e*sta mat-t*ee*na
this afternoon	**questo pomeriggio**
	qu*e*sto pomair*ee*d-jo
tonight	**questa sera**
	qu*e*sta s*e*h-ra
tomorrow	**domani**
	dom*a*n-ee
tomorrow morning	**domani mattina**
	dom*a*n-ee mat-t*ee*na
tomorrow afternoon	**domani pomeriggio**
	dom*a*n-ee pomair*ee*d-jo
tomorrow evening ⎤	**domani sera**
tomorrow night ⎦	dom*a*n-ee s*e*h-ra
the day after tomorrow	**dopo domani**
	d*o*p-o dom*a*n-ee

MONTHS AND DATES

January	**gennaio**
	jen-n*a*h-yo
February	**febbraio**
	feb-br*a*h-yo
March	**marzo**
	m*a*rtzo
April	**aprile**
	apr*ee*leh
May	**maggio**
	m*a*d-jo
June	**giugno**
	j*oo*n-yo
July	**luglio**
	l*oo*l-yo
August	**agosto**
	ag*o*sto
September	**settembre**
	set-t*e*mbreh
October	**ottobre**
	ot-t*o*breh

November	**novembre**
	novembreh
December	**dicembre**
	deechembreh
in January	**in gennaio**
	in jen-nah-yo
until February	**fino a febbraio**
	feeno ah feb-brah-yo
before March	**prima di marzo**
	preema dee martzo
after April	**dopo aprile**
	dopo apreeleh
during May	**durante maggio**
	dooranteh mad-jo
not until June	**non fino a giugno**
	non feeno ah joon-yo
the beginning of July	**l'inizio di luglio**
	lineetzio dee lool-yo
the middle of August	**la metà di agosto**
	la meto dee agosto
the end of September	**la fine di settembre**
	la feeneh dee set-tembreh
last month	**il mese scorso**
	il mez-eh scorso
this month	**questo mese**
	questo mez-eh
next month	**il mese prossimo**
	il mez-eh pros-seemo
in spring	**in primavera**
	in preemavaira
in summer	**in estate**
	in estat-eh
in autumn	**in autunno**
	in ah-ootoon-no
in winter	**in inverno**
	in invairno
this year	**quest'anno**
	questan-no
last year	**l'anno scorso**
	lan-no scorso
next year	**l'anno prossimo**
	lan-no pros-seemo

in 1982	**nel mille novecento ottantadue**
	nel m*ee*l-leh noveh-ch*e*nto ot-tanta-d*oo*eh
in 1985	**nel mille novecento ottantacinque**
	nel m*ee*l-leh noveh-ch*e*nto ot-tanta-ch*i*nqueh
in 1990	**nel mille novecento novanta**
	nel m*ee*l-leh noveh-ch*e*nto nov*a*nta
What's the date today?	**Qual'è la data di oggi?**
	qual-*e*h la d*a*t-ah dee *o*d-jee
It's the 6th of March	**È il sei di marzo**
	eh il say dee m*a*rtzo
It's the 12th of April	**È il dodici di aprile**
	eh il d*o*deechee dee apr*ee*leh
It's the 21st of August	**È il ventuno di agosto**
	eh il vent*oo*no dee ag*o*sto

Public holidays

● On these holidays offices, shops and schools are closed.

1 January	**Primo dell'anno**	New Year's Day
	Capodanno	
...	**Lunedì dell'Angelo**	Easter Monday
25 April	**Anniversario della Liberazione**	Liberation Day
1 May	**Festa dei Lavoratori**	Labour Day
15 August	**Assunzione**	Assumption
1 November	**Tutti i Santi**	All Saints Day
	I Morti	
8 December	**Immacolata Concezione**	Immaculate Conception
25 December	**Natale**	Christmas
26 December	**Santo Stefano**	Boxing Day

COUNTRIES AND NATIONALITIES

Countries

Australia	(l') Australia
	(l) a-oostrul-ya
Austria	(l') Austria
	(l) a-oostree-ah
Belgium	(il) Belgio
	(il) beı-jo
Britain	(la) Gran Bretagna
	(la) gran bretan-ya
Canada	(il) Canada
	(il) canada
East Africa	(l') Africa Est
	(l) africa aist
Eire	(l') Eire
	(l) eh-eereh
England	(l') Inghilterra
	(l) ing-eeltairra
Greece	(la) Grecia
	(la) graıcha
India	(l') India
	(l) ındia
Italy	(l') Italia
	(l) italia
Luxembourg	(il) Lussemburgo
	(il) loos-semboorgo
Netherlands	(i) Paesi Bassi
	(ee) pah-ehzee bas-see
New Zealand	(la) Nuova Zelanda
	(la) nwova zailanda
Northern Ireland	(l') Irlanda del Nord
	(l) eerlanda deı nord
Pakistan	(il) Pakistan
	(il) pakistan
Portugal	(il) Portogallo
	(il) portogaı-lo
Scotland	(la) Scozia
	(la) scotzia
Spain	(la) Spagna
	(la) span-ya

Switzerland	**(la) Svizzera** (la) z*vee*t-tzera
United States	**(gli) Stati Uniti** (l-yee) st*a*t-ee oon*ee*tee
Wales	**(il) Galles** (il) g*al*·les
West Germany	**(la) Germania Ovest** (la) jairman-ya *o*vaist
West Indies	**(le) Indie Occidentali** (leh) *ee*ndi-eh ot-chident*al*-ee

Nationalities
(Use the first alternative for men, the second for women)

American	**americano/americana** american-o/american-ah
Australian	**australiano/australiana** ah-oostral-y*an*-o/ah-oostral-y*an*-ah
Canadian	**canadese** canad*ai*zeh
East African	**est africano/est africana** aist african-o/aist african-ah
English (used for 'British')	**inglese** ingl*ai*zeh
Indian	**indiano/indiana** indi*a*n-o/indi*a*n-ah
Irish	**ir¹andese** irland*ai*zeh
a New Zealander	**neozelandese** nai-odzeland-*ai*zeh
a Pakistani	**pachistano/pachistana** pak¹st*a*n-o/pakist*a*n-ah
Scots	**scozzese** scot-tz*ai*zeh
South African	**sudafricano/sudafricana** soodafrican-o/soodafrican-ah
Welsh	**gallese** gal-l*ai*zeh

West Indian	**indiano occidentale/
	   indiana occidentale**
	indi*a*n-o ot-chident*al*-eh/
	   indi*a*n-ah ot-chident*al*-eh

DEPARTMENT STORE GUIDE

Abbigliamento e accessori neonato-bambini	Babies–children's department
Abbigliamento e attrezzi sportivi	Sports clothing and equipment
Abbigliamento donna	Ladies' fashions
Abbigliamento uomo	Men's fashions
Accessori auto	Car accessories
Accessori bagno	Bathroom accessories
Alimentari	Food
Arredamento (cucine)	Furniture (kitchen)
Articoli da campeggio	Camping equipment
Articoli casalinghi	Household appliances
Articoli fotografici	Photography
Articoli da fumo	Smokers
Articoli da pesca	Fishing equipment
Articoli da pulizia	Cleaning materials
Articoli da regalo	Gifts
Articoli per ufficio	Office equipment
Articoli da viaggio	Travel articles
Biancheria	Linen
Borse(tte), portafogli	Bags, wallets
Bricolage	Do-it-yourself
Calzature	Shoes
Calze	Stockings/socks
Camicie(tte)	Shirts (blouses)
Cartoleria	Stationery
Cinture	Belts
Coperte	Blankets
Corsetteria	Underwear
Cosmetici	Cosmetics
Cotoni	Cottons
Cravatte	Ties
Cristalleria	Crystal
Dischi	Records
Elettrodomestici	Electrical appliances
Ferramenta	Hardware
Fotocopie	Photocopies
Foulards	Scarves
Giocattoli	Toys
Gioielli	Jewellery

Gonne	Skirts
Guanti	Gloves
Impermeabili	Rainwear
Lana	Wool (knitting)
Libri	Books
Maglieria	Knitwear
Mare	Beach clothes
Maternità	Maternity
Mercerie	Haberdashery
Mobili	Furniture
Moda giovane	Young fashions
Modisteria	Millinery
Ombrelli	Umbrellas
Orologi	Watches
Pantaloni	Trousers
Pellicceria	Furs
Piano	Floor
Porcellane	Porcelain
Primo piano	First floor
Profumeria	Perfumery
Quarto piano	Fourth floor
Radio-televisori	Radios–televisions
Ristorante	Restaurant
Sciarpe	Scarves
Secondo piano	Second floor
Seminterrato	Basement
Tacco espresso-chiavi	Heel bar–keys cut
Taglie forti	Outsize department
Tappeti	Carpets
Tende	Curtains
Terzo piano	Third floor
Tessuti	Fabrics
Ufficio informazioni	Information office
Ufficio vendite a credito	Credit sales department
Ufficio viaggi	Travel agency
Vetro-ceramica	Glass–china

CONVERSION TABLES

Read the centre column of these tables from right to left to convert from metric to imperial and from left to right to convert from imperial to metric e.g. 5 litres = 8.80 pints; 5 pints = 2.84 litres.

pints		litres		gallons		litres
1.76	1	0.57		0.22	1	4.55
3.52	2	1.14		0.44	2	9.09
5.28	3	1.70		0.66	3	13.64
7.07	4	2.27		0.88	4	18.18
8.80	5	2.84		1.00	5	22.73
10.56	6	3.41		1.32	6	27.28
12.32	7	3.98		1.54	7	31.82
14.08	8	4.55		1.76	8	36.37
15.84	9	5.11		1.98	9	40.91

ounces		grams		pounds		kilos
0.04	1	28.35		2.20	1	0.45
0.07	2	56.70		4.41	2	0.91
0.11	3	85.05		6.61	3	1.36
0.14	4	113.40		8.82	4	1.81
0.18	5	141.75		11.02	5	2.27
0.21	6	170.10		13.23	6	2.72
0.25	7	198.45		15.43	7	3.18
0.28	8	226.80		17.64	8	3.63
0.32	9	255.15		19.84	9	4.08

inches		centimetres		yards		metres
0.39	1	2.54		1.09	1	0.91
0.79	2	5.08		2.19	2	1.83
1.18	3	7.62		3.28	3	2.74
1.58	4	10.16		4.37	4	3.66
1.95	5	12.70		5.47	5	4.57
2.36	6	15.24		6.56	6	5.49
2.76	7	17.78		7.66	7	6.40
3.15	8	20.32		8.65	8	7.32
3.54	9	22.86		9.84	9	8.23

miles		kilometres
0.62	1	1.61
1.24	2	3.22
1.86	3	4.83
2.49	4	6.44
3.11	5	8.05
3.73	6	9.66
4.35	7	11.27
4.97	8	12.87
5.59	9	14.48

A quick way to convert kilometres to miles: divide by 8 and multiply by 5. To convert miles to kilometres: divide by 5 and multiply by 8.

fahrenheit (°F)	centigrade (°C)		lbs/ sq in	k/ sq cm
212°	100° boiling point		18	1.3
100°	38°		20	1.4
98.4°	36.9° body temperature		22	1.5
86°	30°		25	1.7
77°	25°		29	2.0
68°	20°		32	2.3
59°	15°		35	2.5
50°	10°		36	2.5
41°	5°		39	2.7
32°	0° freezing point		40	2.8
14°	−10°		43	3.0
−4°	−20°		45	3.2
			46	3.2
			50	3.5
			60	4.2

To convert °C to °F: divide by 5, multiply by 9 and add 32. To convert °F to °C: take away 32, divide by 9 and multiply by 5.

CLOTHING SIZES

Remember – always try on clothes before buying. Clothing sizes are usually unreliable.

women's dresses and suits

Europe	38	40	42	44	46	48
UK	32	34	36	38	40	42
USA	10	12	14	16	18	20

men's suits and coats

Europe	46	48	50	52	54	56
UK and USA	36	38	40	42	44	46

men's shirts

Europe	36	37	38	39	41	42	43
UK and USA	14	$14\frac{1}{2}$	15	$15\frac{1}{2}$	16	$16\frac{1}{2}$	17

socks

Europe	38–39	39–40	40–41	41–42	42–43
UK and USA	$9\frac{1}{2}$	10	$10\frac{1}{2}$	11	$11\frac{1}{2}$

shoes

Europe	34	$35\frac{1}{2}$	$36\frac{1}{2}$	38	39	41	42	43	44	45
UK	2	3	4	5	6	7	8	9	10	11
USA	$3\frac{1}{2}$	$4\frac{1}{2}$	$5\frac{1}{2}$	$6\frac{1}{2}$	$7\frac{1}{2}$	$8\frac{1}{2}$	$9\frac{1}{2}$	$10\frac{1}{2}$	$11\frac{1}{2}$	$12\frac{1}{2}$

Do it yourself

Some notes on the language

This section does not deal with 'grammar' as such. The purpose here is to explain some of the most obvious and elementary nuts and bolts of the language, based on the principal phrases included in the book. This information should enable you to produce numerous sentences of your own making.

There is no pronunciation guide in this section, partly because it would get in the way of the explanations and partly because you have to do it yourself at this stage if you are serious - work out the pronunciation from all the earlier examples in the book.

THE

All nouns in Italian belong to one of two genders: masculine or feminine, irrespective of whether they refer to living beings or inanimate objects.

The (singular)	masculine	feminine
the address	l'indirizzo	
the apple		la mela
the bill	il conto	
the cup of tea		la tazza di tè
the glass of wine	il bicchiere di vino	
the key		la chiave
the luggage	(this is only plural in Italian, see below)	
the menu	il menú	
the newspaper	il giornale	
the receipt		la ricevuta
the sandwich	il panino	
the suitcase		la valigia
the telephone directory		la guida telefonica
the timetable	l'orario	
the travel agent's		l'agenzia di viaggi
the zoo	lo zoo	

Important things to remember

- *The* is **il** before most masculine nouns and **la** before feminine nouns.
- *The* is **lo** before certain masculine nouns because of the way they are spelt, notably those which begin with a 'z', e.g. **lo zoo**.
- *The* is **l'** before masculine and feminine nouns which begin with a vowel: **l'indirizzo** (*m*) and **l'agenzia di viaggi** (*f*).
- You can often predict if a singular noun is masculine or feminine by its ending. Masculine nouns usually end in 'o' and feminine nouns in 'a'. But there are several exceptions, notably a whole group of nouns which end in 'e', e.g. **il giornale**, so you should learn and remember all genders. If you are reading a word with **il**, **lo** or **la** in front of it, you can detect its gender immediately: **il menú** and **lo zoo** are masculine (*m*. in dictionaries) and **la valigia** is feminine (*f*. in dictionaries).
- Does it matter? Not unless you want to make a serious attempt to speak correctly and scratch beneath the surface of the language. You would be understood if you said **la menú** or even **il agenzia di viaggi**, provided your pronunciation was good.

The (plural)	masculine	feminine
the addresses	gli indirizzi	
the apples		le mele
the bills	i conti	
the cups of tea		le tazze di tè
the glasses of wine	i bicchieri di vino	
the keys		le chiavi
the luggage	i bagagli	
the menus	i menú	
the newspapers	i giornali	
the receipts		le ricevute
the sandwiches	i panini	
the suitcases		le valigie
the telephone directories		le guide telefoniche
the timetables	gli orari	
the travel agents		le agenzie di viaggi
the zoos	gli zoo	

Important things to remember

- Most masculine nouns in the plural end in 'i' and most feminine nouns end in 'e'.
- *The* is i before most masculine nouns in the plural. However where in the singular *the* is ' or lo, in the plural *the* is gli. [*See two tables above.*]
- *The* is le before all feminine nouns in the plural.
- In Italian. luggage is always regarded as plural. It is never used to mean a singular item.

Practise saying and writing the following sentences in Italian; note that there are two ways of saying *have you got* politely in Italian: ha (when speaking to one person); avete (when speaking to more than one person or in an 'organization', e.g. a hotel, a shop or a tourist information office):

Have you got the key?	**Avete la chiave?**
Have you got the luggage?	**Avete .. ?**
Have you got the telephone directory?	**Ha ... ?**
Have you got the menu?	
I'd like the key	**Vorrei la chiave**
I'd like the receipt	**Vorrei ...**
I'd like the bill	
I'd like the keys	
Where is the key?	**Dov'è la chiave?**
Where is the timetable?	**Dov'è ... ?**
Where is the address?	
Where is the zoo?	
Where is the suitcase?	
Where is the travel agent's?	
Where are the keys?	**Dove sono le chiavi?**
Where are the sandwiches?	**Dove sono ... ?**
Where are the apples?	
Where are the suitcases?	
Where is the luggage?	**Dove sono ... ?**
Where can I get the key?	**Dove posso trovare la chiave?**
Where can I get the address?	**Dove posso trovare ... ?**
Where can I get the timetables?	

Now try to make up more sentences along the same lines.
Try adding please: per favore, at the end.

A/AN

A/an (singular)	masculine	feminine
an address	un indirizzo	
an apple		una mela
a bill	un conto	
a cup of tea		una tazza di tè
a glass of wine	un bicchiere di vino	
a key		una chiave
a menu	un menú	
a newspaper	un giornale	
a receipt		una ricevuta
a sandwich	un panino	
a suitcase		una valigia
a telephone directory		una guida telefonica
a timetable	un orario	
a travel agent's		un'agenzia di viaggi
a zoo	uno zoo	

Some/any (plural)	masculine	feminine
addresses	degli indirizzi	
apples		delle mele
bills	dei conti	
cups of tea		della tazze di tè
glasses of wine	dei bicchieri di vino	
keys		delle chiavi
luggage	dei bagagli	
menus	dei menú	
newspapers	dei giornali	
receipts		delle ricevute
sandwiches	dei panini	
suitcases		delle valigie
telephone directories		delle guide telefoniche
timetables	degli orari	
travel agents		delle agenzie di viaggi
zoos	degli zoo	

Important things to remember

- *A* or *an* is **un** before most masculine nouns and **una** before most feminine nouns.
- Before the group of masculine nouns which start with a 'z', *a* or *an* is **uno**.
- Before feminine nouns which begin with a vowel, *a* or *an* is **un'**.
- *Some* or *any* is:
    dei before most masculine nouns in the plural.
    delle before all feminine nouns in the plural.
- Before masculine nouns in the plural which begin with a vowel, or the 'z' group, *some* or *any* is **degli**.
- In certain expressions in Italian, **dei**, **delle** or **degli** are left out; see an example of this in the sentences marked * below.

Practise saying and writing these sentences in Italian:

Have you got a receipt?	Ha una ricevuta?
Have you got a menu?	Ha ... ?
I'd like a telephone directory	Vorrei ...
I'd like some sandwiches	
Where can I get some newspapers?	Dove posso trovare ... ?
Where can I get a cup of tea?	
Is there a key?	C'è una chiave?
Is there a telephone directory?	C'è ... ?
Is there a timetable?	
Is there a menu?	
Is there a zoo?	
Is there a travel agent's?	
Are there any keys?	Ci sono delle chiavi?
Are there any newspapers?	Ci sono ... ?
Are there any sandwiches?	

Now make up more sentences along the same lines.

Then try these new phrases:

Io prendo ... (I'll have ...)
Avrei bisogno di ... (I need ...)

I'll have a glass of wine	Io prendo un bicchiere di vino
I'll have a cup of tea	Io prendo ...
I'll have some sandwiches	
I'll have some apples	
I need a cup of tea	Avrei bisogno di una tazza di tè
I need a key	Avrei bisogno di ...
*I need some newspapers	Avrei bisogno di giornali
*I need some keys	Avrei bisogno di ...
*I need some addresses	Avrei bisogno di ...
*I need some sandwiches	Avrei bisogno di ...
*I need some suitcases	

SOME/ANY

In cases where *some* or *any* refer to more than one thing, such as *some/any* ice-creams, *some/any* sunglasses and *some/any* bananas, **dei**, **degli** and **delle** are used as explained earlier:

dei gelati	(some/any ice-creams)
degli occhiali da sole	(some/any sunglasses)
delle banane	(some/any bananas)

As a guide, you can usually *count* the number of containers or whole items.

In cases where *some* refers to part of a whole thing or an indefinite quantity, the words **dei**, **degli** and **delle** cannot be used.
Look at the list below:

the bread	il pane	some bread	del pane
the flour	la farina	some flour	della farina
the oil	l'olio (m)	some oil	dell'olio
the sugar	lo zucchero	some sugar	dello zucchero
the water	l'acqua (f)	some water	dell'acqua
the wine	il vino	some wine	del vino

Important things to remember

- del is used for masculine nouns.
- delle is used for feminine nouns.
- dell' is used for both masculine and feminine nouns which begin with a vowel.
- dello is used for the group of masculine nouns which begin with a 'z'.

Can you complete the list below?

the beer	la birra	. . .	some beer
the tea	il tè	. . .	some tea
the lemonade	la limonata	. . .	some lemonade
the aspirin	l'aspirina (*f*)	. . .	some aspirin
the cheese	il formaggio	. . .	some cheese
the coffee	il caffè	. . .	some coffee

Practise saying and writing these sentences in Italian:

Have you got some coffee?	Avete del caffè?
Have you got some flour?	
Have you got some sugar?	
I'd like some aspirin	Vorrei dell'aspirina
I'd like some oil	
I'd like some bread	
Is there any lemonade?	C'è della limonata?
Is there any water?	
Is there any wine?	
Where can I get some cheese?	Dove posso trovare del formaggio?
Where can I get some flour?	
Where can I get some water?	
I'll have some beer	Io prendo della birra
I'll have some tea	
I'll have some coffee	

THIS AND THAT

There are two words in Italian: questo (this), quello (that)

If you don't know the Italian for an object, just point and say:

Vorrei quello	I'd like that
Prendo quello	I'll have that
Avrei bisogno di questo	I need this

HELPING OTHERS

You can help yourself with phrases such as:

I'd like . . . a sandwich	Vorrei . . . un panino
Where can I get . . . a cup of tea?	Dove posso trovare . . . una tazza di tè
I'll have . . . a glass of wine	Io prendo . . . un bicchiere di vino
I need . . . a receipt	Avrei bisogno di . . . una ricevuta

If you come across a compatriot having trouble making himself or herself understood, you should be able to speak to the Italian person on their behalf.

It is not necessary to say the words for *he* (lui), *she* (lei) and *I* (io) in Italian unless you want to emphasize them, e.g. *He'll* have a beer and *I'll* have a glass of wine. (A pronunciation guide is provided from here on, to help you with the unfamiliar parts of each phrase.)

He'd like . . .	(Lui) vorrebbe un panino
	(loo-ee) vorreb-beh oon pan*ee*no
She'd like . . .	(Lei) vorrebbe un panino
	(lay) vorreb-beh oon pan*ee*no
Where can he get . . . ?	Dove può trovare (lui) una tazza di tè?
	dov-eh poo-o trovar-eh (loo-ee) oona *tat*-tza dee teh
Where can she get . . . ?	Dove può trovare (lei) una tazza di tè?
	dov-eh poo-o trovar-eh (lay) oona *tat*-tza dee teh
He'll have . . .	(Lui) prende un bicchiere di vino
	(loo-ee) prendeh oon beec-kee-*ai*reh dee veeno
She'll have . . .	(Lei) prende un bicchiere di vino
	(lay) prendeh oon beec-kee-*ai*reh dee veeno
He needs . . .	(Lui) avrebbe bisogno di una ricevuta
	(loo-ee) avreb-beh beezon-yo dee oona reechev*oo*ta
She needs . . .	(Lei) avrebbe bisogno di una ricevuta
	(lay) avreb-beh beezon-yo dee oona reechev*oo*ta

You can also help a couple or a group if they are having difficulties.
The Italian word for *they* is loro, but it is usually left out altogether.
Look at the verb ending:

They'd like . . .	**(Loro) vorrebbero del formaggio** (loro) vorreb-bero del formad-jo
Where can they get . . . ?	**Dove possono trovare dell'aspirina?** dov-eh pos-sonno trovar-eh del-laspireena
They'll have . . .	**Prendono del vino** prendono del veeno
They need . . .	**Avrebbero bisogno di acqua** avreb-bero beezon-yo dee acqua

What about the two of you? No problem. The word for *we* is noi
(noy), but it is only really important to change the verb ending:

We'd like . . .	**Vorremmo del vino** vorrem-mo del veeno
Where can we get . . . ?	**Dove possiamo trovare dell'acqua?** dov-eh pos-see-am-o trovar-eh del-lacqua
We'll have . . .	**Prendiamo della birra** prendee-am-o della beerra
We need . . .	**Avremmo bisogno di aspirina** avrem-mo beezon-yo dee aspireena

Try writing out your own checklists for these four useful phrase-
starters, like this:

Vorrei . . .	**Vorremmo . . .**
Vorrebbe (lui) . . .	**Vorrebbero . . .**
Vorrebbe (lei) . . .	
Dove posso trovare . . . ?	**Dove . . . trovare . . . ? (noi)**
Dove può trovare (lui) . . . ?	**Dove . . . trovare . . . ? (loro)**
Dove può trovare (lei) . . . ?	

You will find more practice on the next page.

MORE PRACTICE

Here are some more Italian names of things. See how many different sentences you can make up, using the various points of information given earlier in this section.

		singular	plural
1	ashtray	portacenere (*m*)	portaceneri
2	bag	borsa (*f*)	borse
3	car	macchina (*f*)	macchine
4	cigarette	sigaretta (*f*)	sigarette
5	corkscrew	cavatappi (*m*)	cavatappi
6	deckchair	sedia a sdraio (*f*)	sedie a sdraio
7	garage (repairs)	autoriparazioni (*f*)	autoriparazioni
8	grapes	uva (*f*)	(*no plural*)
9	ice-cream	gelato (*m*)	gelati
10	melon	melone (*m*)	meloni
11	passport	passaporto (*m*)	passaporti
12	rag (dishcloth)	straccio (*m*)	stracci
	NB this word takes 'lo' and 'uno'		
13	salad (lettuce)	insalata (*f*)	insalate
14	shoe	scarpa (*f*)	scarpe
15	stamp	francobollo (*m*)	francobolli
16	station	stazione (*f*)	stazioni
17	sunglasses		occhiali da sole (*m*)
18	telephone	telefono (*m*)	telefoni
19	telephone token	gettone (*m*)	gettoni
20	ticket	biglietto (*m*)	biglietti

Index

Travellers' Multilingual Phrase Book £3.99

An up-to-date phrase book developed from the results of a nationwide survey of the needs of modern travellers abroad. An invaluable companion for holiday and business. Languages included: Dutch, French, German, Greek, Italian, Portuguese, Serbo-Croat and Spanish – in one handy volume. Special features: clear, easy-to-use design; pronunciation guide; helpful information on customs and lifestyles of the countries covered; conversion tables; each language's own reference section and index.

Companion Language Dictionaries

Companion
English–Espanol
Spanish–Ingles
Dictionary

Companion
English–Deutsch
German–English
Dictionary

Companion
English–Italiano
Italian–Inglese
Dictionary

The compact bilingual dictionaries are handy, up-to-date
reference books for students, travellers and tourists and are
designed for use by both English *and* French, German, Spanish
and Italian Speakers.

★ Over 400 pages

★ 10,000 headwords and over 35,000 references

★ More idiomatic expressions and contemporary vocabulary
   than comparable dictionaries.

★ Explanation of meanings **preceding** possible translations

★ Grammatical information included where helpful

★ Pronunciation guide to foreign language and English
   headwords

★ £2.50 each

All Pan books are available at your local bookshop or newsagent, or can be ordered direct from the publisher. Indicate the number of copies required and fill in the form below.

Send to: **CS Department, Pan Books Ltd., P.O. Box 40, Basingstoke, Hants. RG21 2YT.**

or phone: 0256 469551 (Ansaphone), quoting title, author and Credit Card number.

Please enclose a remittance* to the value of the cover price plus: 60p for the first book plus 30p per copy for each additional book ordered to a maximum charge of £2.40 to cover postage and packing.

*Payment may be made in sterling by UK personal cheque, postal order, sterling draft or international money order, made payable to Pan Books Ltd.

Alternatively by Barclaycard/Access:

Card No.

Signature:

Applicable only in the UK and Republic of Ireland.

While every effort is made to keep prices low, it is sometimes necessary to increase prices at short notice. Pan Books reserve the right to show on covers and charge new retail prices which may differ from those advertised in the text or elsewhere.

NAME AND ADDRESS IN BLOCK LETTERS PLEASE:

....

Name ————————————————————————————————

Address ——————————————————————————————

————————————————————————————————————

————————————————————————————————————

————————————————————————————————————

3/87